SPECTRUM
Spelling

Grade 6

Published by Spectrum
an imprint of Carson-Dellosa Publishing LLC
Greensboro, NC

Spectrum
An imprint of Carson-Dellosa Publishing LLC
P.O. Box 35665
Greensboro, NC 27425 USA

Printed in the U.S.A. • All rights reserved.   ISBN 978-0-7696-5266-5

06-087118454

Table of Contents Grade 6

Table of Contents, continued

Pronunciation Key and Sample Words

0/a/ = admire, canyon

/ā/ = bouquet, rain

/ä/ = garage, macaroni

/â/ = repair, stair

/e/ = lemon, method

/ē/ = field, receive

/ê/ = deer, year

/i/ = distance, strict

/ī/ = height, kite

/o/ = comedy, modern

/ō/ = open, plateau

/ô/ = explore, report

/oi/ = moist, spoil

/ou/ = mountain, mouth

/u/ = clumsy, hundred

/ū/ = review, value

/ü/ = attitude, reduce

/ù/ = football, nook

/û/ = disturb, purchase

/ch/ = merchant, purchase

/ng/ = length, young

/sh/ = establish, friendship

/th/ = nothing, truth

/th/ = brother, clothing

/hw/ = buckwheat, overwhelm

/zh/ = pleasure, sage

/ə/ = a = another, national

e = effect, label

i = habit, pencil

o = observe, original

u = up, crust

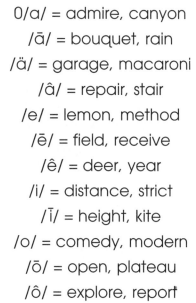

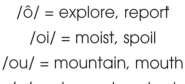

Lesson 1 Short Vowels: a, e, i

Say each of the following words out loud, stressing the short vowel sounds. Then, write each word.

> **Spelling Tip**
>
> Short **a** is spelled **a**, short **e** is spelled **e** and **ea**, short **i** is spelled **i**. The symbol for short **a** is /a/. The symbol for short **e** is /e/. The symbol for short **i** is /i/,

Spelling Words

animal   _____

except   _____

distance   _____

canyon   _____

meadow   _____

install   _____

fantastic   _____

mention   _____

skill   _____

fraction   _____

method   _____

strict   _____

grand   _____

pleasant   _____

swimming   _____

Lesson 1 Short Vowels: a, e, i

Words in Context

Complete the paragraph below with spelling words.

Rocky Mountain National Park

In the middle of the splendor of the Rocky Mountains is one of America's most beautiful national parks. Visitors are amazed by the wild nature that surrounds them year-round. Don't be surprised if you

encounter an _____ in the park. Elk, deer, moose, bighorn sheep, black bears, coyotes, cougars, eagles, and hawks are common.

In the summer, a grassy

_____ or hillside will show off their alpine wildflowers. Climbers can tackle challenging peaks. The park is home to 60 peaks with the elevation

Challenge

Circle the other words in the paragraph that have short **a**, **e**, and **i** sounds.

starting at a _____ of 8,000 feet and going all the way to 14,259 feet.

Climbers with much _____ can climb over the tree-line. They are awed

by a _____ view of a _____ below. Trail Ridge Road, at 12,183 feet, is the highest continuous paved road in the United States.

In the summer, campers and backpackers enjoy the _____

surroundings of the wilderness. All year long, visitors can enjoy _____ wildlife viewing. Rocky Mountain National Park is a park for all ages and abilities.

Word Building

A **gerund** is a verb form that ends in **ing** and is used as a noun. For example, the verb *write* can become a gerund when it is changed to *writing*. One spelling word can be a gerund. Write the word and its definition.

Word: _____   Definition: _____

Lesson 1 Short Vowels: a, e, i

Fun with Words
Complete the crossword puzzle with spelling words.

Across

1. The mathematical expression $\frac{2}{3}$ is called a _____.
3. The reporter told the artist he would _____ his name in the newspaper review.
4. The warm breeze coming off the ocean was a _____ ending to the evening.
7. The members of the track and field team had a _____ training schedule.

Down

2. The service technician was called to _____ the new telephone.
3. A _____ is a way of doing something or a process.
5. Holly liked all fruit _____ for raspberries.
6. _____ was Mikka's favorite sport.

Words Across the Curriculum
Write the social studies words on the lines.

1. discoveries _____ 3. excavation _____

2. evidence _____ 4. historic _____

Complete the following paragraph with the social studies words.

A Career as an Archaeologist

Do you like digging in the earth and making _____? If so, then

archaeology may be for you. Archaeologists study _____ people and

places. They go on an _____ to find _____ from the past.

Lesson 1 Short Vowels: a, e, i

Words in Writing

Write a paragraph about what career you want to have when you grow up. Use at least four words from this lesson.

_____

_____

_____

_____

_____

_____

_____

_____

Misspelled Words

Each of the following sentences has a misspelled spelling word. Cross out the misspelled word and write the word correctly above it.

1. A medow is a low, level grassland near a lake or stream.

2. Rocky Mountain National Park is the home to many anamals.

3. A friction has both a numerator and a denominator.

4. The word exceapt can be a preposition, a verb, or a conjunction.

5. Swiming is one of the best forms of exercise.

6. A canyen is a long, narrow valley with high cliffs on each side.

7. Evedence is something that gives reasons or proof.

8. Scientists have made many important descovorys.

9. A citation made to honor or praise is an honorable meantion.

10. The distence of a marathon is 26.2 miles.

Lesson 2 Short Vowels: o, u

Say each of the following words out loud, stressing the short vowel sounds. Then, write the words on the lines provided.

> **Spelling Tip**
>
> The short **o** sound can be spelled **o**. The short **o** sound can also be spelled **au**, **aw**, **oa**, and **ough**. These spelling are called *digraphs*. They have slightly different sounds. The symbols for short **o** are /o/ and /ô/ (for the digraphs). The short **u** sound is spelled with the letter **u**. The symbol for short **u** is /u/.

Spelling Words

comedy   _____

clumsy   _____

audience   _____

hundred   _____

awkward   _____

husband   _____

broad   _____

reluctant   _____

sought   _____

stumble   _____

modern   _____

public   _____

auditorium _____

understand _____

awning   _____

Lesson 2 Short Vowels: o, u

Words in Context

Complete the following sentences with spelling words.

1. The box was both tall and _____.

2. After graduation, the students _____ jobs in their fields.

3. Please be careful and don't _____ on the ice as you leave the auditorium.

4. The play goers waited under the _____ to avoid the rain.

5. An _____ moment followed after the actress momentarily forgot her lines.

6. At first, the children were _____ to go into the water.

7. Instead of antiques, the couple was looking for _____ furniture.

8. The parents could _____ their children's initial reluctance.

9. When my brother got married, he became a _____.

10. Everyone in the school had to go to the _____, because there was a pep rally for our basketball team.

11. I've always wanted to be in a play. My favorite kind of play is a _____.

12. We had a math test today. I got ninety-five right out of one _____.

13. After Sonia and I finished our magic show and the curtain closed, we were nervous.

    The clapping and cheering that came from the _____ made us smile.

14. In the play, *The Crazy Clown*, the title character tripped over everything. He was

    extremely _____.

15. There were three dress rehearsals for the new play. But on opening night, the

    theater's doors were opened to the _____.

Lesson 2 Short Vowels: o, u

Fun with Words

Complete this set by choosing spelling words to fill-in the blanks on the stage and the blanks in the dialogue.

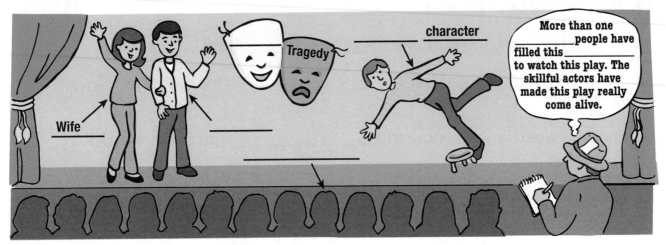

Words Across the Curriculum

Write the science words on the lines beside each word.

1. clusters _____

2. phenomenon _____

3. spawn _____

4. thunderstorms _____

5. unstable _____

Complete the following paragraph with science words from above.

Thunderstorms

_____ are an extremely common weather _____.

Thunderstorms can be only a few miles in diameter or can form _____

that cover hundreds of miles. They usually occur in warm, humid conditions, although

dry thunderstorms are common in the western United States. Dry thunderstorms can

_____ wildfires. When the air in a thunderstorm becomes

_____, or likely to quickly change, the storms can cause sever damage.

However, only 10% of thunderstorms in the U.S. become this strong.

Lesson 2 Short Vowels: o, u

Words in Writing

Write a paragraph about a natural phenomenon. Use at least six words from this lesson.

_____

_____

_____

_____

_____

_____

_____

_____

_____

_____

_____

_____

Using a Dictionary

Words in a dictionary are listed alphabetically. Write the spelling words alphabetically.

_____   _____   _____

_____   _____   _____

_____   _____   _____

_____   _____   _____

Review Lessons 1–2

Write each of the following words on the lines provided. Then, circle the letter or letters that give each word the short **a**, short **e**, or short **i** sound.

1. animal _____

2. except _____

3. meadow _____

4. distance _____

5. fantastic _____

6. method _____

7. pleasant _____

8. swimming _____

Complete the following narrative with words from above.

Claude and Todd were excited. They had been taking _____ lessons for years. Their school had a big meet this coming Saturday. Their coach had

taught them a new exercise _____, and they felt they were getting

stronger. They had also been practicing going a longer _____ than they would be required for the meet. They rode their bikes to school together on Saturday morning.

They passed an _____ in a green _____ along the way. It seemed as if the pretty horse was wishing them well. It looked like it would be a

_____ day. They just hoped they felt the same way after the meet.
Everyone in the gymnasium was excited. Claude and Todd warmed up. The whistle blew and they hit the water. It was cold but that helped spur them on. Claude

felt strong. Todd felt good, _____ for a cramp he developed in his side. They both did well. Their relay team came in first, Claude had one other first-place finish and two second-place finishes. Todd had two second-place finishes and one

third. They both knew they had done their best. They had a _____ day.

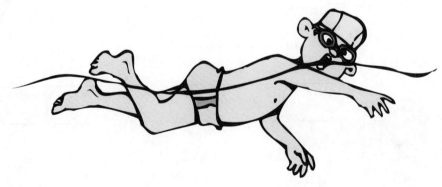

Review Lessons 1-2

Write each of the following spelling words. Then, circle the letter or letters that make this word have the short **o** or short **u** sound.

1. comedy _____ **6.** clumsy _____

2. auditorium _____ **7.** modern _____

3. awkward _____ **8.** reluctant _____

4. broad _____ **9.** audience _____

5. sought _____ **10.** awning _____

Words from the above list are misspelled in the sentences below. Correctly rewrite the words on the lines after each sentence.

1. From the sound of the applause, the awdience must have loved the movie.

_____

2. Some of the students wore vintage clothes to the party, and some wore moadern attire.

_____

3. The graduate students saught an apartment with three bedrooms and a large kitchen.

_____

4. The uniform was too big and felt aukward to wear.

_____

5. The couple couldn't decide if they wanted to see a coamedy or a drama.

_____

6. The awditorium was not going to be large enough for the reception.

_____

7. The football player had broghd shoulders.

_____

8. The awkward chef was going to start his own television show, *The Clomsy Cook*.

_____

9. The students were relauctant to start the long test.

_____

10. The sign on the auning announced the opening of the new play.

_____

Lesson 3 Long Vowels: **a**, **e**, **i**

Say each of the following words out loud, stressing the long vowel sounds. Then, write the words on the lines provided.

Spelling Tip	Long **a** can be spelled **a**, **ai**, **ay**, **ea**, **eigh**, and **a-consonant-e**. The symbol for long **a** is /ā/. Long **e** can be spelled **ea**, **ee**, **ei**, **ie**, and **y**. The symbol for long **e** is /ē/. Long **i** can be spelled **i**, **igh**, **y**, and **i-consonant-e**. The symbol for long **i** is /ī/.

Spelling Words

behavior _____

maintain _____

display _____

clean _____

freight _____

escape _____

season _____

chimpanzee _____

receive _____

achieve _____

velocity _____

migrate _____

bright _____

reply _____

prize _____

Lesson 3 Long Vowels: a, e, i

Words in Context

Complete the following paragraph with spelling words.

Chimp Life

When you look at pictures of an ape,

a gorilla, or a _____, do they look like they're looking right back and thinking about something? Well, most likely they are. Scientists have proven that chimpanzees are very

intelligent and _____. They have their own communication system. Scientists learned that studying chimpanzees in their own habitat was much better than in laboratories. In the field, scientists could study their true

_____ and habits. Chimpanzees live in groups and communicate to work together. If one chimp finds a food supply, he may jump in the trees and hoot to let others know where

to go. Staying _____ is important to chimps. Grooming each other

communicates friendship. Chimpanzees also _____ affection for one

another with hugs. Other chimps _____ with hugs, kisses, or hand shakes.

Chimpanzees use their sounds, gestures, and facial expressions to _____ communication with other chimps and with people, too. Scientists have taught chimpanzees to use sign language and the computer.

It's unfortunate that some of these intelligent and sensitive animals are in jeopardy. The forests where chimpanzees live are being destroyed. With help from conservation groups and protection agencies, hopefully the chimpanzees will

_____ danger and prosper in their environments.

Lesson 3 Long Vowels: **a, e, i**

Fun with Words

Find seven spelling words in the following poem. Then, write the words under their appropriate categories. One word is used twice.

> With the approaching season
> The fleas planned to migrate
> To a more temperate climate
> Their tans they must maintain.
>
> With swift velocity they sent
> Their freight by way of the skies
> The southern relatives would receive
> Their northern cousins as a prize.

Long **a**   Long **e**   Long **i**

_____   _____   _____

_____   _____   _____

_____   _____

Words Across the Curriculum

Write the social studies words on the lines.

1. body _____   **4.** lakes _____

2. chain _____   **5.** seaway _____

3. great _____

Circle the letters in the social studies words that make the long **a**, **e**, or **i** sounds.

The Great Lakes consist of a chain of five lakes in Canada and the United States. The five lakes are Lake Erie, Lake Huron, Lake Michigan, Lake Ontario, and Lake Superior. These five lakes form the largest body of freshwater in the world. The lakes cover 95,000 square miles. The lakes were formed when the glaciers melted at the end of the Pleistocene period. In 1959, the St. Lawrence Seaway opened, connecting the Great Lakes with the Mississippi River and the Gulf of Mexico. This made the lakes an international body of water. The Great Lakes not only provide transportation for industry, but also areas of great beauty in their parks.

Lesson 3 Long Vowels: a, e, i

Words in Writing

Write a poem or short story about nature using at least five of the spelling words.

_____

_____

_____

_____

_____

_____

_____

_____

_____

Misspelled Words

Some of the spelling words are misspelled in the following paragraph. Cross out any misspelled words and rewrite them correctly above the misspelled word.

Why Do Animals Migrate?

Migration means that animals move from one location to another. Animals usually mighgrate due to the changing of a seeson. Some animals need to escaip colder climates. They are looking to mayntayn food and water supplies that come with warmer temperatures. Some animals in dry regions migreight to escap droughts. Migration may not always be necessary for adult animals, but babies need ideal conditions to acheive the best care. Therefore, reproduction is most often the primary reason for seasonal migrations.

Lesson 4   Long Vowels: o, u

Say each of the following words out loud, stressing the long vowel sounds. Then, write the words on the lines provided. Over emphasize the difference between the /ū/ and the /ü/.

Spelling Tip	Long **o** can be spelled **o, oa, ow,** and **o-consonant-e**. The symbol for long **o** is /ō/. Long **u** has two sounds. The /ū/ sound is spelled **u** and has a **y** sound at the beginning of the vowel. The /ü/ sound is spelled **u, ue, ew, oo, ou, u-consonant-e,** and **ui-consonant-e**. The difference between /ū/ and /ü/ is slight.

Spelling Words

condominium _____

coast _____

below _____

mole _____

humid _____

studio _____

blue _____

drew _____

cartoon _____

troupe _____

attitude _____

toast _____

growth _____

universe _____

costume _____

Lesson 4 Long Vowels: o, u

Words in Context

Homographs are words that are spelled the same but have different meanings. Use spelling words to complete the following sentences. The words you use will be used twice for different meanings of the same word. Then, after you complete each sentence, write your own sentence using the word in the same context.

1. When you're going downhill, you can _____ on your bicycle.

   _____

2. The _____ builds its home underground.

   _____

3. Timothy sat down and _____ a picture of a mountain range.

   _____

4. The team felt _____ after losing the tournament.

   _____

5. My cousins live by the ocean, right on the _____ .

   _____

6. You should have that _____ on your shoulder checked by a doctor.

   _____

7. When the knight saw the dragon, he _____ his sword.

   _____

8. Her favorite color is _____ .

   _____

Lesson 4 Long Vowels: o, u

Fun with Words

The following picture contains six spelling words. Look at the picture and then complete the sentences below.

Mr. and Mrs. Frances live in a _____ on the beach. They like living

on the _____ of the ocean. Mr. Frances likes _____ for

breakfast. Mrs. Frances likes to read a _____ in the newspaper before

she eats. Mr. Frances is an artist and has a _____ upstairs. Mrs. Frances is

a clothes designer who always has a _____ hanging in her closet.

Words Across the Curriculum

Write the language arts words on the lines.

1. newspaper _____

3. produced_____

2. poet   _____

4. wrote   _____

Complete the following paragraph with the language arts words.

During the 1920s, African American writers and artists _____ many works of literature and art. Langston Hughes was a Harlem Renaissance

_____ whose poems often used dialects and jazz rhythms. He

_____ mainly of urban African-American life. In addition to poetry,

Hughes wrote plays, children's books, novels, and _____ articles. Langston Hughes is considered one of the world's greatest and most influential writers.

Lesson 4 Long Vowels: o, u

Words in Writing

Create a cartoon strip. Draw figures inside each square and put dialogue in bubbles coming from the characters' mouths. Use at least four words from this lesson.

Using the Dictionary

The difference between the /ü/ and the /ū/ sounds can seem quite slight. However, when you pronounce the words carefully, you can hear a difference. The /ü/ sounds like ōō, while the /ū/ sounds like yōō. There are many more spellings for yōō, as you learned in this lesson. Using a dictionary write the pronunciations of the following spelling words.

1. attitude _____
2. blue _____
3. cartoon _____
4. drew _____

5. humid _____
6. studio _____
7. troupe _____
8. universe _____

NAME _____

Review Lessons 3–4

Write each of the following spelling words. Then, circle the letter or letters that make each word have the long **a**, long **e**, or long **i** sound.

1. behavior _____
2. freight _____
3. maintain _____
4. achieve _____
5. chimpanzee _____

6. receive _____
7. season _____
8. bright _____
9. prize _____
10. reply _____

Complete the following sentences with words from above.

1. The principal told the students to be on their best_____ during the pep rally.

2. Her dream was to _____ a medal in track and field.

3. The sun was _____, and the clouds were moving away.

4. The _____ was transported by ship.

5. The students were studying the behavior of the gorilla and the _____.

6. The best _____ at the fair was the stuffed teddy bear.

7. The students went to summer school to _____ their spelling skills.

8. Charlie was hoping to _____ at least a B+ on his English paper.

9. Billy was waiting for a _____ from his college applications.

10. Autumn was quickly approaching, the _____ of pumpkins and falling leaves.

Spectrum Spelling
Grade 6
24

Review
Lessons 3–4

Review Lessons 3-4

Write each of the following spelling words. Then, circle the letter or letters that make each word have the long **o** and long **u** sound.

1. condominium _____

2. coast _____

3. below _____

4. universe _____

5. studio _____

6. blue _____

7. influential _____

8. newspaper _____

Complete the advertisements below with words from above.

Classified Advertisements

FOR SALE

We have a beautiful two bedroom _____ for sale. This condo is located in an _____, well-landscaped neighborhood. The breakfast nook looks out onto the ocean _____. The living room has vaulted ceilings and a fireplace. The basement is perfect for an office or a workout room. You'll love the abundance of closet space. Contact the number listed in this _____ for more information on this find of the _____!

FOR RENT

We have an attractive _____ apartment for rent. This apartment is perfect for one person with an artistic flair. The skylights let in the sun and a view of _____ skies. A cozy kitchen is nestled beside the bedroom area. The fortunate renter receives free admission to the art gallery _____ the apartment. Call the number listed in the _____ quickly, because this one will go fast!

LESSONS 3-4 REVIEW

Lesson 5 Consonants Digraphs: **ch**, **ph**, **sh**, **th**, **wh**

Say each of the spelling words out loud. Then, write each word.

Spelling Tip	Consonant digraphs are two or more consonant letters that together make one specific sound. Say each of the following consonant digraphs: **ch**, **ph**, **sh**, **th**, **wh**.

Spelling Words

champion _____

alphabet _____

accomplish _____

athletic _____

wheat _____

check _____

photo _____

finish _____

marathon _____

when _____

chocolate _____

physical _____

shutter _____

thousand _____

wheeze _____

Lesson 5 Consonants Digraphs: **ch, ph, sh, th, wh**

Words in Context
Complete the following article with spelling words. Not all of the words will be used, and some words will be used more than once.

What is a marathon?

A _____ is a long distance foot race.

How long is a marathon?
A marathon is 26.2 miles.

How did the marathon get its name?
The marathon received its name from the city of Marathon, Greece. According to legend, in 490 B.C. a runner named Pheidippides ran from Marathon to Athens, Greece (approximately 26 miles) carrying news of a battle victory over the Persians.

_____ **was the first official race?**
To celebrate the feat of Pheidippides, the first modern Olympics in 1896 held the first official marathon, retracing Pheidippides's route.

Who runs marathons?

Olympians train for marathons, as well as other professional athletes. But you don't

have to be a _____ to run marathons today. As running became more popular, recreational runners became interested in marathons as training for

_____ fitness, to achieve personal goals, and to test endurance. Today, tens of thousands of runners participate in marathons. What is thought of as a small

race may have more than a _____ runners. It is still considered to be a

_____ of athletic skill, with less than one percent of the world's

population ever completing a marathon. Many people would _____ to think of running more than just a few miles, let alone more than 26 miles. It takes

incredible _____ and mental conditioning and training. But for those who have accomplished this task, all of the efforts more than pay off when crossing

the _____ line.

Lesson 5 Consonants Digraphs: **ch**, **ph**, **sh**, **th**, **wh**

Fun with Words

The bowl of soup contains all of the letters you will need to spell nine of the spelling words. Pick out and arrange the letters on the spoons below to spell out the nine words. You can use the letters more than once, but you cannot add letters.

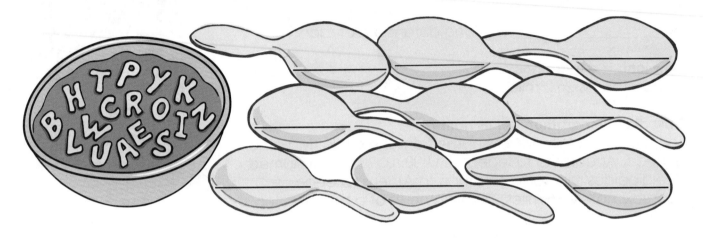

Words Across the Curriculum

Write the social studies words on the lines. Use a dictionary if you need help defining any of the words.

1. empathy _____   **3.** whisperer _____

2. friendship _____

Complete the following paragraph with words from above.

A Horse Whisperer

Buck Brannaman is a horse _____ _____. He has revolutionized the world

of horse training and has paved the way for other trainers to follow. Brannaman's

methods do not include "breaking in" a horse. His techniques involve forming trust

and _____ with his horses. He shows _____, a sharing of

emotions and feelings. The horses respond and bonds are formed. Brannaman believes

that listening to his horses is the best way to form a bond with them.

Lesson 5 Consonants Digraphs: **ch, ph, sh, th, wh**

Words in Writing

Write a paragraph about your friendship with a classmate, relative, or animal. Use at least five words from this lesson.

_____

_____

_____

_____

_____

_____

Misspelled Words

The following recipe contains misspelled spelling words. Cross out the words that are misspelled and rewrite them correctly above the misspelled words.

No Bake Champion Chokolate Oatmeal Cookies

2 cups	sugar	1 teaspoon	vanilla
3 tablespoons	cocoa	1 cup	coconut
½ cup	vegetable oil	3 cups	oatmeal
½ cup	2% milk		

If you decide to make this recipe, be sure you have adult supervision.

Mix sugar, coca, vegetable oil, and milk in a 2 quart glass bowl. Bring the

mixture to a soft boil in the microwave for one minute. Add the remaining ingredients

and stir. Drop by spoonfuls onto wax paper. Finihs by letting cool. Anyone can

accomplich making these champhion chocolate cookies. Sprinkle with powdered

sugar and have your camera ready for the perfect dessert foto!

Lesson 6 Double Consonants

Say each of the words out loud. Then, write each word on the lines provided.

Spelling Tip	Words with double consonants are often misspelled. Take extra time to remember how to spell those words.

Spelling Words

address   _____

afford   _____

announcement   _____

broccoli   _____

college   _____

committee   _____

community   _____

compassion   _____

dilemma   _____

excellenl   _____

mirror   _____

necessary   _____

possess   _____

puzzle   _____

recess   _____

Lesson 6 Double Consonants

Words in Context

Complete the following sentences using spelling words.

1. Make sure the _____ is correct on the envelope before mailing it.

2. Let's jump rope at _____.

3. Can we _____ the new car?

4. I like to work the crossword _____ in the newspaper.

5. The students _____ many reading and math skills.

6. The _____ of the new principal will be made at the next meeting.

7. Is it _____ to fill out all of the forms?

8. _____ is a very healthful vegetable.

9. Look in the _____ before going out on stage.

10. My brother is going to play basketball in _____ this year.

11. You received an A on your paper; that is an

    _____ grade.

12. The homecoming _____ will vote on the decorations at their next meeting.

13. Having both play and baseball practice on the

    same night poses quite a _____.

14. Have you completed your _____ service project yet?

15. The students have shown much _____ to the animals we visited in the shelters.

Lesson 6 Double Consonants

Fun with Words

Write the spelling word that matches each of the pictures represented below.

1.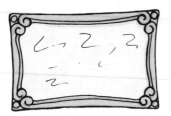

_____

3.

_____

5.

Al White
289 Rivermill Loop
Boston, MA 20000

_____

2.

Mitchell High School
presents:
The Music Man
May 1st-4th
Call Now For Tickets!

_____

4.

_____

6.

_____

Words Across the Curriculum

Write the history words on the lines. Use a dictionary if you need help defining any of the words.

1. battles _____

3. successful _____

2. officer _____

4. surrender _____

Complete the following biography with the history words from above.

Commodore Oliver Perry

Oliver Hazard Perry didn't know he would become a national hero when he

became an American naval _____ in 1799. During the War of 1812,
between the U.S. and England, Perry's fleet left Put-In-Bay, Ohio, and encountered

a British fleet. Perry and his sailors were _____ in forcing the British to

_____. Perry's victory allowed the U.S. to take control of Lake Erie and

led to the success of future _____ during the war.

Lesson 6 Double Consonants

Words in Writing

Write a dialogue with at least two characters. Write about a school event, an athletic event, a family event, or a community service project. Use at least six words from this lesson in your dialogue.

_____

_____

_____

_____

_____

_____

Using the Dictionary

Sometimes, a word will have more than one definition. Look up the following words in a dictionary. Write the definitions that match the use of the words in Words in Context on page 31.

1. address:_____

2. announcement: _____

3. afford:_____

4. committee: _____

5. community: _____

6. compassion:_____

7. dilemma: _____

8. necessary:_____

9. possess: _____

10. recess:_____

Lesson 7 Silent Letters: **bt**, **ck**, **gu**, **mn**, **sc**

Say each of the spelling words out loud. Then, write each word on the lines provided.

Spelling Tip	Sometimes, letter combinations produce silent letters. Say each of the following letter combinations with silent letters: **bt** (only the **t** is pronounced), **ck** (only the **k** is pronounced), **gu** (only the **g** is pronounced), **mn** (only the **n** is pronounced), and **sc** (only the **s** is pronounced).

Spelling Words

debt   _____

ascend   _____

autumn   _____

guardian   _____

nickel   _____

doubt   _____

scenic   _____

column   _____

intrigue   _____

pocket   _____

subtle   _____

science   _____

solemn   _____

league   _____

rocket   _____

Lesson 7 Silent Letters: **bt**, **ck**, **gu**, **mn**, **sc**

Words in Context

Complete the following paragraph with spelling words.

A Career in Space

Imagine yourself soaring into the sky. As you

_____, you are above the clouds and into space.

What a _____ view! If thoughts of traveling in

_____ ships really interest you, then you should consider a career in the space industry. If you would like to follow in the footsteps of Neil Armstrong, John Glenn, and

Mae Jemison, you can start by studying _____, math, and even physical fitness in school. Space scientists must know a lot about biology, chemistry, physics, and mathematics. Those individuals who are fortunate enough to go into space must also

be physically fit. _____ differences in physical ability can make a huge difference in successfully completing a training program.

If you love reading about space, but _____ you're the type to walk on the Moon, plenty of careers are still open to you. Chemists, engineers, computer scientists, mathematicians, and even writers can all have careers full of

_____ that deal with space. Writing a newspaper _____ can make an astronaut famous. Most people who pursue a career in space, do so for

the love of science and space. Joining the _____ of space scientists in any capacity would be a rewarding life long career.

Word Building

Antonyms are words that mean the opposite of each other. Use a thesaurus or dictionary to find at least one antonym for each of the following spelling words.

1. ascend _____

2. autumn _____

3. doubt _____

4. solemn _____

5. subtle _____

Lesson 7 Silent Letters: **bt**, **ck**, **gu**, **mn**, **sc**

Fun with Words

Unscramble the speling words on each leaf and rewrite them on the lines provided.

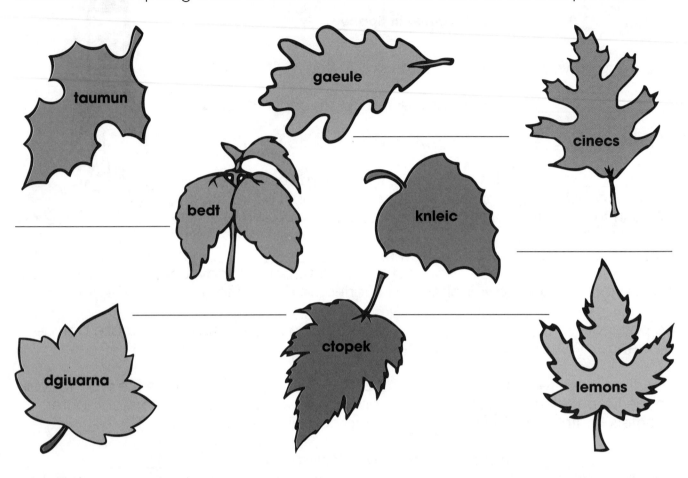

taumun

gaeule

_____

cinecs

bedt

knleic

_____

_____

_____

dgiuarna

ctopek

lemons

_____   _____   _____

Words Across the Curriculum

Write the social studies words on the lines beside each word.

1. guidance _____   **3.** scholarships _____

2. schedule _____

Complete the following sentences with words from above.

1. The _____ counselors have many responsibilities.

2. They are responsible for helping students attain _____.

3. They also help students with their daily _____.

Lesson 7 Silent Letters: **bt**, **ck**, **gu**, **mn**, **sc**

Words in Writing
Write a paragraph about a community service project you have either worked on or would like to work on. Use at least five spelling words.

_____

_____

_____

_____

_____

_____

_____

Misspelled Words
The following sentences contain misspelled spelling words. Cross out the misspelled words and write them correctly at the end of each sentence.

1. After he received a raise, the borrower was happy to pay off his dept. _____

2. Danny became a happy gardian of a shepherd mix puppy for the humane society. _____

3. While out on a walk, Karl found one quarter, two dimes, and a nikel. _____

4. Rory and Betsy decided to take the senic route along the river on their way home. _____

5. The table consisted of a dozen rows and a single colum. _____

6. The movie was full of suspense and intrige. _____

7. Marissa liked the poket on the jeans. _____

8. Brian was determined to join the baseball leage. _____

Review Lessons 5–7

Write each of the following spelling words. Then, circle the consonant digraphs.

1. champion _____

2. chocolate _____

3. photo _____

4. physical _____

5. accomplish _____

6. finish _____

7. athletic _____

8. marathon _____

9. wheat _____

10. when _____

Complete the following paragraph with words from above.

Louis Tucker was very _____. His dream was to be a

_____ in the state track and field event. He was willing to do whatever it

took to succeed. His _____ fitness was very important. He trained every

day. He watched his diet. His favorite food was whole _____ pasta.

_____ the event was over, if all went well, he would reward himself

with his favorite treat, _____ ice cream. Louis was very goal oriented.

After finishing school, he dreamed of completing his first _____. He could

just picture the _____ of himself crossing the _____ line

now. Louis had dreams to _____ quite a lot.

Review Lessons 5–7

Write each of the following spelling words. Then, circle the double consonants.

1. broccoli _____

2. college _____

3. committee _____

4. community _____

5. compassion _____

6. mirror _____

7. puzzle _____

8. recess _____

Write the word that matches each description using words from the list above.

1. *a break from study* or *a hollow place in a wall* _____

2. *a question or a problem* or *a game of skill and cleverness* _____

3. *a vegetable* _____

4. *a place of higher studies or specialized training* _____

5. *a surface that reflects light* _____

6. *the need to help others* _____

7. *a group of people that studies and/or plans events* _____

8. *a place where all of the people of a certain area live* or *a group of people who share common interests* _____

Write each of the following spelling words. Then, circle the letter combination that forms the silent combination.

1. autumn _____

2. guardian _____

3. rocket _____

4. scenic _____

5. solemn _____

6. subtle _____

Lesson 8 Vowel Diphthongs: **oi**, **oy**, **ou**, **ow**

Say each spelling word out loud. Then, write each word on the lines provided.

Spelling Tip	**Vowel diphthongs** are combinations of vowels that make a specific sound. This sound can be identified when comparing the following spelling words to each other. Some common vowel diphthong combinations are: **oi** and **oy** and **ou** and **ow**. The **oi** and **oy** diphthongs share a common sound and **ou** and **ow** share a common sound.

Spelling Words

appointment   _____

coil   _____

coin   _____

joint   _____

choice   _____

employ   _____

enjoy   _____

oyster   _____

royal   _____

cloud   _____

house   _____

mountain   _____

crowd   _____

shower   _____

tower   _____

Lesson 8 Vowel Diphthongs: oi, oy, ou, ow

Words in Context

Complete the following paragraph with words from the spelling word list.

A Career in Physical Therapy

Have you ever thought about a job in physical therapy? People are staying

active longer. What does this mean to our joints? Each _____ may wear

down, and an _____ with a physical therapist may be in order.
Physical therapists, by working with joints and muscles, help patients to move better

and feel better. The _____ outlook for the field of physical therapy is quite
good. Physical therapists work at hospitals, clinics, universities, corporations. They also
have practices of their own. They work directly with injured people and their families.
Not only is education important but physical therapists must also be kind and
compassionate.

If you _____ working with people and are good at science,

physical therapy may be a good career _____ for you.

Word Building

Suffixes are groups of letters that are added to the ends of words to change their
meanings. The suffix -**ment** means *action, process,* or *condition.* Write the spelling word
that has the -**ment** suffix and define it. Then, add the suffix -**ment** to two other spelling
words and define the new words.

Word: _____ Definition: _____

_____

Word: _____ Definition: _____

_____

Word: _____ Definition: _____

_____

Lesson 8 Vowel Diphthongs: oi, oy, ou, ow

Fun with Words

Find the words from the box in the word search below. Words can be horizontal, vertical, diagonal, forward, and backward.

coil	house
coin	mountain
oyster	crowd
royal	shower
cloud	tower

m	d	w	o	r	c	m	c
o	y	s	t	e	r	o	o
u	u	n	c	h	i	k	i
n	i	h	n	l	s	c	n
t	d	u	o	l	c	o	o
a	t	r	l	u	r	z	b
i	w	e	b	a	s	b	y
n	b	u	n	g	y	e	e
r	e	w	o	t	e	o	z
s	h	o	w	e	r	z	r

Words Across the Curriculum

Write the social studies words on the lines beside each word.

1. boycott _____

2. powerful _____

3. voice _____

Complete the following paragraph with words from above.

What Is a Boycott?

A _____ is the act of refusing to buy, sell, or use something. A historical example of a boycott is when the American colonists in 1765 avoided buying British goods after the passage of the Stamp Act.

The boycott of the Stamp Act worked. It was revoked in 1766. Today, people may boycott certain products if they don't agree on they way they are produced. For example, some people may boycott buying clothes if the manufacturers do not treat

their employees well. Boycotts give a _____ to the public in a

nonviolent, yet potentially _____ way.

Lesson 8 Vowel Diphthongs: oi, oy, ou, ow

Words in Writing

Write a paragraph about a school issue or an issue within your community. Use at least six words from this lesson.

_____

_____

_____

_____

_____

_____

Using the Dictionary

When looking up a word in a dictionary, you use **guide words** to help find the word you are looking for on the page. The guide words are the first and last word on a dictionary page. They are usually found on the top of each dictionary page. If the word you are looking for is between the two guide words, then it will be on that page. Look up the following words in a dictionary. Write the spelling word and then write the guide words on the lines provided.

1. appointment _____   _____   _____

2. coil _____   _____   _____

3. employ _____   _____   _____

4. house _____   _____   _____

5. joint _____   _____   _____

6. mountain _____   _____   _____

7. oyster _____   _____   _____

8. royal _____   _____   _____

9. shower _____   _____   _____

10. tower _____   _____   _____

Lesson 9 — r-Controlled Vowels: **ar, er, ir, or, ur**

Say each of the spelling words out loud. Then, write each word.

Spelling Tip	The vowels **a, e, i, o,** and **u** can all be influenced by the letter **r** following them. Words with a **vowel+r** spelling make their own single-syllable sounds, with the **r** sound emphasized more than the vowel.

Spelling Words

department   _____

determine   _____

stir   _____

director   _____

bureau   _____

larger   _____

pattern   _____

first   _____

historical   _____

disturb   _____

wardrobe   _____

serve   _____

inspiration   _____

humorous   _____

urban   _____

Lesson 9 r-Controlled Vowels: **ar, er, ir, or, ur**

Words in Context

Each of the spelling words are scrambled below. Unscramble them, and then write them on the line.

Five isHtrolica _____ Figures:
a reformer, an inventor, a politician, a poet, and a scientist

Henry Bergh – reformer (1811–1888)

Henry Bergh grew up in a rich and influential family. But something became more important to him than money. He felt awful when he saw animals overworked, neglected, or abused.

He wanted to terdemine _____ a solution and make a difference. It wasn't an easy task; he had to sidburt

_____ authorities and rsti _____ up

favors from friends. In 1866, he opened the irfts _____ organization in the United States to protect animals and enforce animal protection laws. This organization became known as the *American Society for the Prevention of Cruelty to Animals* (ASPCA). In 1874, Bergh created the Society for the Prevention of Cruelty to Children. Helping

those in need was a tternpa _____ all throughout his life.

George Washington Carver – inventor and scientist (1864–1943)

George Washington Carver began life as a slave and went on to become one of the most influential men of the 20th century. Carver received his college degree after earning his freedom

from slavery. He became the rectordi _____ of

the rtDemepant _____ of Agricultural Research at Tuskegee University, a job he held his entire life. Carver devoted himself to bettering the economic conditions of the southern United States, specifically the welfare of African Americans. He is best known for his work with peanuts. He invented hundreds of uses for the peanut, as well as sweet potatoes, soybeans, and cotton.

Lesson 9 r-Controlled Vowels: ar, er, ir, or, ur

Shirley Chisholm – politician (1924–2005)

Shirley Chisholm was the first African-American woman to be elected to the United States Congress. She served from 1969 to 1982. Before becoming a congresswoman, she was a consultant

to the New York City eauruB _____ of Child Welfare. Chisholm was recognized nationally as an advocate for the nabur

_____ poor. She was also the first woman to make

a serious attempt to vsere _____ as president of the United States in the 1972 election.

Paul Laurence Dunbar – poet and novelist (1872–1906)

Paul Laurence Dunbar was the first African-American poet to receive international acclaim. Dunbar wrote hsuuomor

_____ poems about African-American life in the southern United States as well as many short stories, song lyrics, and novels. Dunbar's mother served as an nionistpair

_____ to him. Although the Dunbar family did not have material wealth, they were rich in family support and a love of literature.

Albert Einstein – scientist (1879–1955)

Albert Einstein, born in Germany in 1879, was the first scientist to gain international popularity and fame. He won the Nobel Peace Prize for Physics in 1921. He was a pacifist, and he loved sailing and the violin. He was known to keep a small brodearw

_____ so as not to spend much time deciding what to wear. After his death, Einstein's brain was preserved and studied. It was discovered that part of his brain was missing, and

that another section had grown arlegr _____. The section that grew larger is responsible for mathematical thought.

Lesson 9 r-Controlled Vowels: **ar, er, ir, or, ur**

Words in Writing

Write a biography about a historical figure who you admire. Use at least five of the words from the spelling word list.

_____

_____

_____

_____

_____

_____

_____

Misspelled Words

Find the misspelled spelling words in the following sentences. Rewrite the words correctly on the lines provided.

1. Elise lived in a rural environment and Rebecca lived in an urbon setting.   _____

2. Don't forget to stur the soup every few minutes.   _____

3. The movie had a very humerous ending.   _____

4. A boreau can be an agency that provides information or service, or it can be a chest of drawers.   _____

5. Lionel's fourth grade teacher was a real insperation to him.   _____

6. The movie was made to disterb its audiences.   _____

7. The students wanted to surve their community by participating in fundraising projects.   _____

8. Judith wanted to shop for a new spring wordrobe.   _____

Lesson 10 The /ə/ Sound

Say each word out loud. Then, write each word on the lines provided.

Spelling Tip	The /ə/ sound is an unaccented vowel. It can be found in any part of a word.

Spelling Words

exceptional   _____

camel   _____

castle   _____

identical   _____

easel   _____

dazzle   _____

mineral   _____

label   _____

example   _____

original   _____

level   _____

people   _____

sandal   _____

tunnel   _____

visible   _____

Lesson 10 The /ə/ Sound

Words in Context
Complete the paragraph below with spelling words. The first letter of each word has been provided for you.

Neuschwanstein Castle

Do you think that Cinderella's Castle at Disney World in Florida is an

o_____? Cinderella's Castle was

patterned after a real c_____ in Germany—the Neuschwanstein Castle.
King Ludwig of Germany began construction on his castle in 1869. The

e_____ castle is

v_____ as it peeks through the towering Alps that surround it. It is an

e_____ of the Romanesque style with its turrets, balconies, and one

l_____ above another. The interior is not i_____ to the

castle in Florida, but it will d_____ the eye. The castle is filled with

priceless murals, woodcarvings, and ornaments. Thousands of p_____ visit the castle every year.

Word Building
Synonyms are words that have the same or similar meaning. Choose spelling words that are synonyms for the following words. Use a thesaurus or dictionary if you need help.

1. outstanding = _____

2. enchant = _____

3. exact = _____

4. model = _____

5. flat = _____

6. genuine = _____

7. passage = _____

8. noticeable = _____

Lesson 10 The /ə/ Sound

Fun with Words

An easel is a stand that holds an artist's canvas. The pictures on each canvas represent a spelling word. Write the correct spelling word underneath each easel.

1.

_____

3.

_____

5.

_____

2.

_____

4.

PO#5678
Cartons: 1
Product: 1
Tunnel Art
Ship To:
John Doe
PO Box 123
Detroit, MI 98765

_____

6.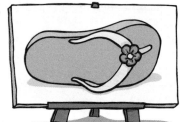

_____

Words Across the Curriculum

Write the social studies words on the lines beside each word.

1. bottles _____

3. recycle _____

2. natural _____

4. vegetable _____

Complete the following paragraph with words from above.

_____ means *to make waste reusable*. The average American household throws away 13,000 paper items, 500 aluminum cans, 500 glass

_____, and 1,800 plastic items every year. You can help by recycling those items instead of throwing them away in the trash. You can recycle other items

besides those, too. Even _____ peelings can be saved and used on

lawns as a _____ way to fertilize. Talk to your parents and set up a recyling plan in your home. The planet will thank you for it.

Lesson 10　The /ə/ Sound

Words in Writing

Write ten sentences below, using a different word from this lesson in each.

1. _____

2. _____

3. _____

4. _____

5. _____

6. _____

7. _____

8. _____

9. _____

10. _____

Using the Dictionary

Some vowels in unaccented syllables are represented by /ə/, called *schwa*. Look up the pronunciations of the following spelling words in a dictionary and write the phonetic respellings on the lines provided. Notice where the /ə/ is in each word.

1. camel _____

2. castle _____

3. easel _____

4. label _____

5. mineral _____

6. natural _____

7. original _____

8. recycle _____

9. sandal _____

10. tunnel _____

11. vegetable _____

12. visible _____

Lesson 11 Words with **ci** and **ti**

Say each of the words out loud. Then, write them on the lines provided.

Spelling Tip	Sometimes, the letters **ci** and **ti** make the /sh/ sound.

Spelling Words

ancient _____

immunization _____

commercial _____

infection _____

efficient _____

innovation _____

especially _____

introduction _____

glacier _____

portion _____

social _____

production _____

sufficient _____

question _____

vaccination _____

Lesson 11 Words with **ci** and **ti**

Words in Context
Complete the following paragraph with spelling words.

Vaccination

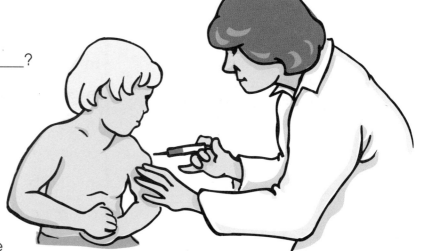

What is a _____?

Do you know the answer to that

_____?
Vaccination is a means of producing immunity against certain diseases through the

_____ of living or dead antibodies. In this way, the

body's _____ of less dangerous antibodies fights an_____.

Vaccinations were used in _____ times in China, India, and Persia.

Edward Jenner proved that injecting just a small _____ of a virus into the

skin was _____ to defend the body against viruses. This

_____ wiped out small pox and can prevent many other diseases.

_____, which means to protect against disease _____
through vaccination, of 12 different diseases is recommended for children. Researchers

are working to make a more _____, one-dose vaccine for many diseases.

Word Building
Antonyms are words that have the opposite or close to the opposite meanings of each other. Write the spelling words that are antonyms for the following words. Use a thesaurus or dictionary if you need help.

1. modern = _____

2. time-consuming = _____

3. whole = _____

4. not enough = _____

Lesson 11 Words with ci and ti

Fun with Words

Find and circle the spelling words in the word search puzzle. They can be horizontal, vertical, forward, backward, and diagonal.

Words Across the Curriculum

Write the social studies words on the lines beside each word.

1. distribution _____

2. information _____

3. nation _____

4. occupation _____

5. official _____

6. population _____

Complete the following paragraph with words from above.

The Census

Do you know the

_____ ____ of your city or

state? These figures are calculated

with a census. A census is an _____ count of the number of people in a

city, state, or _____. Other _____ gathered includes the

age, gender, ethnicity, and _____ of people in a specific area. The

information gathered is used for a variety of purposes, including the _____

of federal money. A census is taken every ten years in the United States.

c	p	m	a	y	o	r	s	g	s	c	o
o	r	m	i	d	n	i	l	n	o	t	e
m	o	g	h	t	s	a	o	n	r	m	u
m	d	m	a	r	c	i	a	n	n	c	h
e	u	t	h	i	t	v	t	o	k	i	n
r	c	o	e	r	n	a	n	i	b	u	z
c	t	r	o	k	o	c	e	t	z	b	u
i	i	p	s	n	a	c	i	a	b	u	n
a	o	c	o	o	l	i	c	z	g	e	e
l	n	u	c	m	b	n	i	i	w	e	b
t	n	e	i	c	n	a	f	n	b	y	s
u	s	o	a	h	m	t	f	u	t	a	n
a	r	a	l	t	h	i	e	m	l	e	y
q	u	e	s	t	i	o	n	m	m	o	l
o	n	s	m	d	g	n	w	i	e	s	t
i	n	f	e	c	t	i	o	n	o	r	y
n	o	i	t	a	v	o	n	n	i	g	o
e	s	p	e	c	i	a	l	l	y	o	d
n	o	i	t	c	u	d	o	r	t	n	i
s	u	f	f	i	c	i	e	n	t	z	b

Lesson 11 Words with **ci** and **ti**

Words in Writing
Write a commercial of your own. Advertise one of your favorite products, such as your favorite tennis shoes, book, or movie. Use at least four words from this lesson.

_____

_____

_____

_____

Misspelled Words
The following commercial contains misspelled spelling words. Cross out the misspelled words and write them correctly above the misspelled words.

Cruise Comercil

(close-up of a woman wearing a heavy jacket, as she speaks the camera pulls

back and shows her standing near a big glasher)

Woman: Trying to decide on your next vacation? The sun and the beach just isn't

the thing for you? The perfect vacation destination is waiting epecially for you.

(the woman is walking on the decks of a ship—glaciers behind her)

The grandeur of Alaska, with its antient glaciers, amazing populasion of wildlife, and

beautiful mountain peaks are right at your fingertips aboard the Midnight Sun Cruise Ship.

(shots of grizzly bears, moose, and gray wolves; shots of mountain peaks)

(interior shots of the cruise ship: dining room, pool, lounge chairs on deck)

When you're not in port enjoying the unique Alaskan towns and villages, you will be

dining and relaxing aboard our effitient ocean liner. That is if you can pull yourself away

from the decks. The sightseeing never ends, especially here in the land of the midnight sun.

(shot of Midnight Sun Cruise Ship's oficial logo)

Review Lessons 8–11

Write each of the following spelling words on the lines provided. Then, circle the vowel diphthongs and the **r**-controlled vowel combinations.

1. coin _____

2. royal _____

3. house _____

4. mountain _____

5. tower _____

6. wardrobe _____

7. service _____

8. first _____

9. humorous _____

10. disturb _____

Complete the following narrative with words from the list above.

High up on a _____ lived Princess Katrina. She was the only daughter

of a _____ family. She had everything a young princess could ask for: a

beautiful _____, many books, and extravagant jewels. But she was lonely.

She spent most of her time alone in her room high in a castle _____.
One day, she heard laughter outside. The five students below were reading a

_____ play and laughing together. Princess Katrina wished she could live

in a normal _____ and go to a normal school. She quickly ran out of the
castle and met the students on the path.
Princess Katrina pretended to be a new student in town. They told her about the

community play they were all in. It was a play about a silver _____

found outside of a castle. Something seemed to _____ the students,
though. She found out that they were missing one person for their play. "I am at your

_____," said Princess Katrina. She then decided to tell them who she
really was.

At _____, the students were angry, but they realized that she was
lonely and just wanted to have friends. Now, she had five friends!

Review Lessons 8-11

Write each of the following spelling words on the lines provided. Then, circle the letter combinations that make the /sh/ sound.

1. mineral _____
2. camel _____
3. example _____
4. original _____
5. tunnel _____
6. castle _____
7. ancient _____
8. immunization _____
9. glacier _____
10. question _____

Complete the following sentences with words from above.

1. A _____ mark is a punctuation mark used at the end of a sentence.

2. A _____ is a substance formed in the ground by nature, such as quartz, granite, and salt.

3. A large mass of ice and snow is called a _____.

4. An animal that can store food and water for up to a few days is a

   _____.

5. A vaccination is a form of _____.

6. The first of its kind is an _____.

7. People who lived long ago are said have lived in _____ times.

8. A large building that is home to kings and queens is a _____.

9. A train or car traveling in a passage underground is traveling in a

   _____.

10. An _____ is a sample that explains a general rule.

Lesson 12 Compound Words

Say each of the following words out loud. Then, write each word on the lines provided.

Spelling Tip	Compound words combine two complete words to make another word.

Spelling Words

backyard   _____

birdbath   _____

butterfly   _____

classmate   _____

classroom   _____

everybody   _____

everyone   _____

everywhere   _____

hallway   _____

homeroom   _____

hummingbird   _____

outside   _____

summertime   _____

teamwork   _____

wildlife   _____

Lesson 12 | Compound Words

Words in Context

Complete the following sentences using the spelling words.

1. We have many birds, squirrels, and chipmunks in our _____.

2. Our class visited the _____ rehabilitation center on a field trip.

3. It took _____ to complete this huge project.

4. The _____ in the backyard gives the birds a place to drink and bathe.

5. It's fun to play outside in the _____.

6. Did you see that _____ flutter by?

7. Let's play _____ while it is still light out.

8. My _____ and I will complete the assignment together.

9. The _____ moves so swiftly he is sometimes hard to see.

10. Can _____ work on the same report at the same time?

11. I go to _____ first thing in the morning when I get to school.

12. _____ must take their seat before class can begin.

13. The _____ is quiet when class is in session.

14. The _____ is full of busy students.

15. _____ we look, we see examples of beautiful nature.

Lesson 12 Compound Words

Fun with Words

Label the picture below using spelling words. Then, complete the paragraph describing the picture with other spelling words.

The _____ is the best time to work _____. There is

plenty of _____ to see in the _____. After we go back to

our _____, my _____ and I will tell our teacher about the
animals we saw.

Lesson 12 Compound Words

Words in Writing

Write a paragraph about how you would create and maintain a backyard wildlife habitat. Use at least five words from this lesson.

_____

_____

_____

_____

_____

_____

Using the Dictionary

Look up each individual word and write the definitions to these words and the compound words they make. The first one has been done for you.

1. bird = a warm-blooded animal with wings , two feet, and covered in feathers

bath = the act of washing or dipping in water

birdbath = a bowl with water set outside for birds to bathe in

2. home = _____

room = _____

homeroom = _____

3. summer = _____

time = _____

summertime = _____

4. team = _____

work = _____

teamwork = _____

Lesson 13 Contractions

Say each of the following contractions out loud. Then, write each word on the lines provided.

Spelling Tip	**Contractions** are words that apostrophes (') substitute letters. Most contractions are made from forms of the verb *to be* (such as *is* and *are*); *had* and *have*; *could*, *should*, and *would*; *not*; and the phrase *let us*.

Spelling Words

it's   _____

that's   _____

there's   _____

you're   _____

they've   _____

could've   _____

he'd   _____

she'd   _____

we'd   _____

doesn't   _____

don't   _____

hasn't   _____

mustn't   _____

shouldn't   _____

let's   _____

Lesson 13   Contractions

Words in Context
The following dialogue contains words that could be written as contractions. Change the words to contractions from the spelling word list. Write them above the existing words.

Challenge

Circle the other contractions in this dialogue.

The Big Decision

"Hey Lewis, you are in a big hurry. Where are you going?" yelled Lynda.

"I'm on my way to the post office. Can you come with me? There is one right across the street and it should not take long," answered Lewis.

"I do not see why not. On the way, maybe you can tell me what has you so excited."

"I'm sending in my application to be a junior counselor at camp...finally," replied Lewis. "I could have sent it in sooner, but I waited because I was not sure what area I wanted to help. Mr. DeNune says it is time for us to think more seriously about our futures. We are in middle school, after all."

"You must not keep me in suspense," laughed Lynda.

"Mr. DeNune told me to think about the kind of things I really enjoy."

"Well, that's not hard to figure out," said Lynda. "You like baseball."

"I am going to help the kids in little league. That is my idea of a good job. My dad has not been happy that I've been putting off this decision. Now, he'll be glad."

"Well he would be proud of you right now," insisted Lynda.

"They have both got a reason to be proud," said Lynda. "Let us hurry to the post office before it closes."

"We'll make it," claimed Lewis. "It does not close for a half an hour. I'm glad you came along, Lynda."

Lesson 13 Contractions

Fun with Words

Five of the contractions from the spelling word list have been scrambled in this pan.
Use all of the letters and apostrophes to write the five contractions.

_____   _____   _____

_____   _____

Word Building

The following contractions could have two different verbs. For example, *it's* could mean
it is or *it has*. The words and sentences surrounding the word will help you determine
which verb it is. Write the two possible verb choices for the following words. Then, use
them each in a sentence.

1. he's   _____   _____

sentence 1: _____

sentence 2: _____

2. she's   _____   _____

sentence 1: _____

sentence 2: _____

Lesson 13 Contractions

Words in Writing
Write a dialogue between at least two characters. The characters are trying to decide what they would like to do over summer vacation. Use at least six of the contractions from this lesson.

_____

_____

_____

_____

_____

_____

_____

Misspelled Words
Some of the contractions in the following sentences are either misspelled or the apostrophe is in the wrong place. Cross-out the incorrect words and write them correctly on the lines provided.

1. Lets' go to the library on our way home from school.   _____

2. We couldv'e ordered pasta, but we decided
on a pizza instead.   _____

3. This book has very small writing and it dosen't have
any pictures.   _____

4. Shoud'nt we go to the earlier movie, since we have
a game in the morning?   _____

5. Maybe we should change our plans. I here ther's
going to be a storm tomorrow evening.   _____

6. The teacher will check to make sure youre signed
up for the field trip.   _____

Review Lessons 12–13

Write each of the following spelling words on the lines provided.

1. backyard _____

6. homeroom _____

2. classmate _____

7. outside _____

3. classroom _____

8. summertime _____

4. everywhere _____

9. teamwork _____

5. hallway _____

10. wildlife _____

Complete the following sentences with words from above.

1. Don't miss the bus or you may be late for _____.

2. Buddy went to the national park to see and learn about the _____ that inhabits it.

3. Jason's _____ Sharon sits beside him in social studies class.

4. The school _____ is very crowded in between classes and at lunch.

5. Bert looked _____ for his lost keys.

6. The students decorated their _____ for the spring festival.

7. Mora planted flowers and trees, and placed a bird feeder and birdbath in her

_____.

8. Alexie runs a lemonade stand in the _____.

9. Since it stopped raining, the students went _____ for recess.

10. Practice and _____ are necessary to build a successful sports team.

Review Lessons 12-13

Write each of the following spelling words on the lines provided.

1. it's _____

2. that's _____

3. you're _____

4. they've _____

5. he'd _____

6. she'd _____

7. doesn't _____

8. don't _____

9. hasn't _____

10. mustn't _____

11. shouldn't _____

12. let's _____

Complete the following sentences with words from above.

1. The travelers _____ know which way to turn, so they will have to stop for directions.

2. My mother said _____ pick me up after play rehearsal.

3. _____ meet at the park Saturday morning.

4. "_____ going to bring water and snacks, aren't you, Mrs. Sopela?" asked Sarah.

5. If we buy the movie tickets early, we _____ have to wait in line.

6. The weather reporter said _____ supposed to be nice all weekend.

7. We _____ be late for our first day of classes.

8. Mr. Griss said _____ take our class on a field trip next month.

9. My sister _____ decided yet if she wants to play softball or run track.

10. Marty _____ like chocolate ice cream; he prefers strawberry.

11. My aunt and uncle said _____ a cabin we can visit this summer.

12. I told my parents my plans for a summer job, and they said _____ a good idea.

Lesson 14 Regular Plurals

Say each of the following plurals out loud. Then, write each word on the lines provided.

Spelling Tip	Most plurals are made by adding **s** to the singular form. Words that end **consonant+y** change the **y** to **i** and add **es**. Words that end in **vowel+o** add **s**. Words that end in **consonant+o** add **es**. Words the ending in **f** or **fe** and have the /f/ sound in its plural add **s**. Words the end in **f** or **fe** and have the /v/ sound in it is plural change the **f** to **ve** and add **s**.

Spelling Words

letters   _____

thousands   _____

databases   _____

languages   _____

cities   _____

dictionaries   _____

libraries   _____

flamingoes   _____

studios   _____

dominoes   _____

volcanoes   _____

reefs   _____

staffs   _____

bookshelves   _____

calves   _____

Lesson 14 Regular Plurals

Words in Context
Complete the following paragraph with spelling words.

Libraries

Did you know that there are _____ of libraries in

_____ all around the world. Public _____ have large

reference sections with encyclopedias, periodicals, and _____. You can

even find historical essays, journals, and _____ in libraries. They also have

access to the Internet and large computer _____. Want to know about

the world's active _____? Do you know where to find coral

_____? Want to find out information on all kinds of animals, including

_____ and _____? Do you want to learn how to play

_____? You can find all these answers at a library.

Books in many _____ can typically be found in college libraries.

College libraries also sometimes have audio _____ where visitors can
listen to CDs and audiotapes.

Special libraries are run by corporations,
governments, and organizations. Some
libraries are solely devoted to one subject
area. Regardless of the type of library you
visit, they all have rows and rows of

_____.

The excellent _____
at every library are very helpful and are
always willing to help you find the
information you are looking for.

Lesson 14 Regular Plurals

Fun with Words

See how many of the dominoes you can knock over by answering the riddle inside of each box with a spelling word

Our insides are alphabetized and defined. ____	Oceans and borders may change us, but anyone can learn more than one of us. ____	Many famous photographers, artists, and actors have passed through us. ____	We are sat on by very smart and interesting objects. ____	We're oblong on the outside and dotted on the inside. ____

Words Across the Curriculum

Write the social studies words on the lines beside each word.

1. airplanes _____

2. beavers _____

3. eagles _____

4. ferries _____

5. wolves _____

Complete the following paragraph with words from above.

The Wolves of Isle Royale

Imagine trying to cross an enormous lake with no _____ or

_____. That would be pretty hard. Fortunately for a female wolf during the winter of 1948–1949, the lake froze. The wolf crossed Lake Superior to Isle Royale,

Michigan. Now, there are three packs of _____ there. These wolves prey on the moose of the island. In fact, the island is well known for its 45-year predator-prey study. The island, a designated wilderness area, is also home to bald

_____, ospreys, and _____.

Lesson 14 Regular Plurals

Words in Writing
Write five riddles whose answers are words from this lesson.

_____

_____

_____

_____

_____

_____

_____

_____

_____

_____

Using the Dictionary
Below are five words from this lesson and their singular forms that end in the letter **f**.
Look up the singular and plural forms in the dictionary and write their pronunciations.

1. bookshelf: _____

bookshelves: _____

2. calf: _____

calves: _____

3. reef: _____

reefs: _____

4. staff: _____

staffs: _____

5. wolf: _____

wolves: _____

Lesson 15 Irregular Plurals

Say each of the following plurals out loud. Then, write each word on the lines provided.

Spelling Tip	Some words do not have a regular plural form. These words must be memorized.

Spelling Words

children   _____

geese   _____

men   _____

mice   _____

oxen   _____

people   _____

media   _____

women   _____

bass   _____

cod   _____

deer   _____

moose   _____

salmon   _____

sheep   _____

trout   _____

Lesson 15 Irregular Plurals

Words in Context

Cross out the singular words that should be plural and write the correct plural spelling word above them. Some words are used more than once.

Woman dress in their fanciest clothes. Man even wear tuxedoes. The child, both boys and girls, dazzle the crowds. They are ready for their walk down the red carpet. Who are they? They are the actors, writers, directors, producers, and craftspeople who are nominated for an Emmy award. Millions of person from all over the world watch the Emmy award presentations on television. The Emmy awards are given to those professionals who have shown excellence in television. The Emmy's Hall of Fame includes over 100 man and woman. These person have made a significant impact on how television, of all the medium, has changed the lives of the mass audiences who view it.

Lesson 15 Irregular Plurals

Fun with Words

The clues below tell you who is talking in this wilderness scene. The names of the animals are scrambled in the sentences. Unscramble the spelling words to answer the questions.

1. Whether one fish or more, we go by the

   name cdo _____, and we are large fish found in the northern seas.

2. If one of us has wondered off, we'd be a goose, but when we're swimming

   together, we're called egese _____.

3. We're large animals who live in northern regions and whether one or more, we're

   called somoe _____.

4. We live in the ocean but swim up river to lay our eggs. One of us, as well as a

   group of us, is called a lamosn _____.

5. One or more, we're called pehes _____, and we're related to goats.

6. One small rodent with small ears and a long, thin tail is called a mouse, but when

   we're with our friends, we're called cemi _____.

7. We're a small fish in the salmon family who live in lakes, streams, and rivers. One or

   more, we're called rotut _____.

8. We can run swiftly through the woods and whether we're alone or together,

   we're called rede _____.

9. We can live in freshwater or saltwater, and whether one or more of us are

   swimming in the North American waters, we're called sabs _____.

10. One of us is called an ox, but more than one of a group of farm animals is called

    xeno _____.

Lesson 15 Irregular Plurals

Words in Writing
Write five sentences using a different spelling word in each.

1. _____
2. _____
3. _____
4. _____
5. _____

Words Across the Curriculum
Write the social studies words on the lines beside each word.

1. bread _____ 4. corn _____

2. wheat _____ 5. rye _____

3. barley _____

In the paragraph below, cross out the incorrect plural spellings and write them correctly above it.

Food can vary greatly from one region of the world to the

next. However, one food that almost every culture has in

common is bread. Breads was critical to ancient civilizations

because it could be made in the summer and stored all winter.

During the Stone Age, people crushed the grains of barleys and wheats with

stones. Breads was such an important part of the lives of the Egyptians that they buried

loaves in Egyptian tombs. When early American settlers lacked the wheats and ryes

grains of Europe, the Native Americans taught them how to make bread from corns.

Lesson 16   Possessives

Say each of the following possessives out loud. Then, write each word on the lines provided.

Spelling Tip	**Possessives** show possession, or ownership. To spell the possessive of a singular noun, add an apostrophe and an **s**. To spell the possessive of plural nouns ending in **s**, add an apostrophe after the **s**. If the plural noun does not end in an **s**, add both the apostrophe and an **s**.

Spelling Words

coach's   _____

coaches'   _____

director's   _____

directors'   _____

guide's   _____

guides'   _____

player's   _____

players'   _____

referee's   _____

referees'   _____

roommate's   _____

roommates'   _____

student's   _____

students'   _____

teeth's   _____

Lesson 16 Possessives

Words in Context

Cross out the possessives with the incorrectly placed apostrophes and rewrite them correctly above the incorrect words. Underline the spelling words that are used correctly.

Dear Celina,

How are you? I'm writing to you from the end of my first week at summer camp. Both of my roommate's closets are bigger than mine. But they've been here before and had first pick. Sisters can share rooms. Next year, you'll be old enough to come, too. We have many activities to choose from. We're even going to put on a play. I didn't get off to a great start with the director though. At practice last night, I sat in the directors' chair. He was nice about it, though.

My favorite activity so far has been softball. Our first game was yesterday. By the second inning, it was pouring rain. All of the player's uniforms were covered in mud. One of the referees' shirts was so muddy you couldn't tell the white strips from the black ones. All of the referees' whistles blew water—it was funny. My team played really well and won by two runs. We poured a pitcher of water on our coachs' jacket after we won the game. But I don't think he minded—he was really muddy, too. Both coaches' families came to watch our game so we had support.

I've also enjoyed our nature hikes. I'm learning a lot about the environment. Someday, I would like to be a guide, too. Our nature guides' son came along with us. It's amazing how much he knows!

See you in a week!

Love, *Jeanine*

Lesson 16 Possessives

Fun with Words
Choose spelling words that complete the following sentences and fit in the boxes. Write the words in the boxes. Don't forget the apostrophes.

1. The _____ grades got better after he was told he couldn't play basketball.

2. The _____ good condition can be attributed to daily care and proper dentist visits.

3. Charlotte's _____ desk was always cluttered.

4. The _____ association made sure their members were honest and fair in all games.

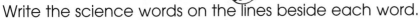

Words Across the Curriculum
Write the science words on the lines beside each word.

1. animal's _____   **3.** male's _____

2. moose's _____

Insert an apostrophe to correct the spelling words below.

What animals body is large and brown and has front legs that are larger than its back legs? It is a moose. A moose is the largest member in the deer family. A mooses habitat is in northern parts of Eurasia and North America. An adult males weight can reach 1,800 pounds. A moose is protected in the national parks and reserves of both the United States and Canada.

Lesson 16 Possessives

Words in Writing

Write a letter to your best friend. Tell your friend about school, family, or community events. Use at least five words from this lesson.

_____

_____

_____

_____

_____

_____

_____

_____

Using the Dictionary

Adding the possessive **'s** to a word gives the word the same sound as its plural form. Some words add an /s/ sound, as in *coach's*. Other words add a /z/ sound, as in *guide's*. Use a dictionary to look up and write the phonetic spellings of each word. Say the word out loud and add either an **s** or a **z** to the end of the phonetic spellings to add the possessive sound. The first one has been done for you.

1. coach's   kōch' əs _____

2. coaches' _____

3. director's _____

4. directors' _____

5. guide's _____

6. guides' _____

7. player's _____

8. players' _____

9. referee's _____

10. referees' _____

11. roommate's _____

12. roommates' _____

13. student's _____

14. students' _____

15. teeth's _____

Review Lessons 14-16

Write each of the following spelling words on the lines provided. For the regular plurals, circle the **s** or **es** that makes the word plural. Do not circle anything in the irregular plurals.

1. thousands _____

2. libraries _____

3. studios _____

4. volcanoes _____

5. reefs _____

6. bookshelves _____

7. children _____

8. geese _____

9. mice _____

10. people _____

11. salmon _____

12. sheep _____

The words from the above list are misspelled in the following paragraph. Cross out the misspelled words and rewrite them correctly above the misspelled word.

Thousandes of peoples visit school librarys every year. They scour the bookshelfs looking for information on everything from accordions to volcanos. One student is going to be a veterinarian and open an animal sanctuary and wildlife rehabilitation center. She uses the library to study geeses, cows, pigs, sheeps, mices, and fish, like salmons. Another student is studying education. He wants to help childrens who have disabilities. He's going to be a coach for the Special Olympics. Another student wants to go into marine biology. He wants to help protect the whales and other sea life. Currently, he is studying the oceans reeves. Yet another student is studying different languages. She uses the audio and video studioes to watch and listen to foreign language dialogues. She wants to teach languages in other countries. Libraries are available to everyone to study and learn. Then, those who learn can teach others who will also benefit from the library system.

Review Lessons 14–16

Write each of the following spelling words on the lines provided. Circle the apostrophe or the **'s** that make each word possessive.

1. coach's _____

2. coaches' _____

3. guide's _____

4. guides' _____

5. player's _____

6. players' _____

7. roommate's _____

8. roommates' _____

9. student's _____

10. students' _____

The words in the above list are scrambled in the following sentences. Unscramble them and write them on the lines provided. Do not forget the apostrophes.

1. Kay likes borrowing her only mormotase' _____ clothes.

2. The four torm'eosam _____ kitchen was nicely stocked with soda pop and snacks.

3. The museum d'iguse _____ microphone was not working.

4. All of the nature sedig'u _____ trail maps were always accurate and up to date.

5. The basketball hoc'acs _____ behavior was inappropriate at the game.

6. The yearbook displayed all of the c'ahocse _____ photographs in one section.

7. The golf yepal'rs _____ caddy had been with him for years.

8. Both tennis la'yreps _____ outfits were corporately sponsored.

9. That sudetns't _____ best friend was moving to another state.

10. All of the tedusnst' _____ homework was due first thing in the morning.

Lesson 17 Prefixes: pre-, post-

Say each of the following words out loud. Then, write each word on the lines provided.

Spelling Tip	A **prefix** is a group of letters that is added to the beginning of a base word to change its meaning. The prefix **pre-** means *before*. The prefix **post-** means *after*.

Spelling Words

preamble _____

prearrange _____

precaution _____

precede _____

predate _____

predetermine _____

preface _____

preheat _____

prelude _____

preview _____

postdate _____

postgraduate _____

postpone _____

postscript _____

postwar _____

Lesson 17 Prefixes: pre-, post-

Words in Context

Complete each sentence with a spelling word.

1. If you see a movie ahead of time, you are seeing the _____.

2. The part at the beginning of a document that states its reason is the

   _____.

3. To write a date that is after the current date is to _____ an item.

4. The part that comes before a musical is the _____.

5. Arranging a meeting ahead of time means to _____ the meeting.

6. Adding a note after the signature is adding a _____.

7. The chef will _____ the oven before she's ready to bake the pie.

8. Taking action ahead of time against danger is taking a _____.

9. A class one takes or studies after graduation is a _____ class.

10. The remarks made at the beginning of a book is the _____.

11. To go or come before in time or order is to _____.

12. If an umpire was to _____ the game, he would be delaying it.

13. To decide ahead of time is to _____.

14. After a war is the _____ period.

15. Writing a date that is before the current date is to _____ an item.

Lesson 17 Prefixes: pre-, post-

Fun with Words

Chef Brian must choose the right word from each bottle in order to correctly complete the story. Write the correct word on the lines provided.

1. predetermine | predate

2. postscript | preview

3. precaution | preamble

4. postdate | preheat

5. preface | prearrange

6. postpone | preheat

The chef needs to (1) _____ what he wants to

serve for dinner. First, he needs to (2) _____ the

recipe. He decides to take (3) _____ and

(4) _____ the oven. Oh, no! He forgets to

read the (5) _____ at the beginning of the
recipe and pours his ingredients in a pan before flouring it.

The chef must (6) _____ the dinner until he
has time to start again.

Words Across the Curriculum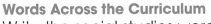

Write the social studies words on the lines beside each word.

1. prehistoric _____   **2.** posthumously _____

Complete the following sentences with words from above. Use a dictionary if you need help.

1. _____ means after something has died.

2. _____ means the time before written history.

Lesson 17   Prefixes: **pre-**, **post-**

Words in Writing
Write eight sentences using a different word from this lesson in each.

_____

_____

_____

_____

_____

_____

_____

_____

Misspelled Words
Some of the words in the following news broadcast are misspelled. Cross out the misspelled words and rewrite the words correctly above the misspelled words.

"Hi! This is Andrea Delmonic standing outside the City Theater. I'm waiting for the audience who is here to prevuw this summer's latest blockbuster to emerge. Here they come now. Excuse me, sir, what do you think of the action-packed musical documentary?"

"It was fantastic! I encourage all future theater goers to prearanje your schedules and buy tickets early."

"Miss, what did you think of this musical set in the postwar period?"

"Don't be late to this one. The pralude is one of the best parts!"

"You heard it here first. Don't postpon seeing this year's biggest movie. I know I won't! This is Andrea Delmonic, entertainment reporter for *Movie News.*"

Lesson 18 Prefixes: im-, in-

Say each of the following words out loud. Then, write each word on the lines provided.

Spelling Tip	The prefixes **im-** and **in-** both can mean *not*.

Spelling Words

imbalance _____

inaccurate _____

immature _____

inactive _____

immeasurable _____

incapable _____

imperfect _____

inconsiderate _____

impossible _____

indecisive _____

impolite _____

indirect _____

improper _____

inexpensive _____

informal _____

Lesson 18 Prefixes: im-, in-

Words in Context

Complete the following paragraph with spelling words. Not all of the words will be used. Words are not used more than once.

Pirates!

Pirates' behavior was seen as _____. They were sometimes known to

be _____. Some people of the time thought them _____

of being upstanding citizens. But many of the reports of these _____

thieves and marauders might have been _____, not necessarily telling
the whole truth.

Many pirates were former navy men. Life in the navy was brutal, and it was

_____ to leave the service once you began. Therefore, if a navy ship
was captured by pirates, some navy men became pirates themselves.

Pirates, who sometimes preferred fancy clothes to _____ ones, had
the opportunity to become rich. Pirates were sometimes hired by governments to raid
ships of opposing countries. These pirates were called *privateers*.

Pirates caused _____ harm to people and property. However,

some positive, _____ benefits did come from piracy. At the time, there

was an _____ in trade throughout the western world, as most goods
were going to a few places. Piracy led to more open trade routes as goods were
taken from one colony to another.

Lesson 18   Prefixes: **im-**, **in-**

Fun with Words

Unscramble the spelling words in the following sentences.

1. The banker concluded that the figures

   were ncuaeiacrt _____.

2. The volcano remained evitcani _____.

3. The pomietil _____ man was

   nosdrteaeinci _____ to others.

4. The T-shirts were relatively inpenexsive _____.

5. The dress for the dance was going

   to be lamrofni _____.

Words Across the Curriculum

Write the science words on the lines beside each word.

1. immersed _____   3. infected _____

2. immobilize _____   4. inhale _____

Complete the following paragraph with words from above. Use a dictionary if you need help.

The medic on the scene had to act quickly when the cyclist in the race fell off his

bike. It looked like his wrist may be broken. First, she made sure to _____
the wrist with a sling. A finger on his other had begun to swell. The medic carefully

_____ his finger in a bucket of ice. Then, she asked him to

_____. This next part was going to hurt a bit. The scratch on his knee

may become _____, and she needed to put alcohol on it. This was
going to sting. But the cyclist was tough.

Lesson 18 Prefixes: im-, in-

Using the Dictionary

Put the words from this lesson in alphabetical order. Then, write a brief definition for each.

1. _____ _____

2. _____ _____

3. _____ _____

4. _____ _____

5. _____ _____

6. _____ _____

7. _____ _____

8. _____ _____

9. _____ _____

10. _____ _____

11. _____ _____

12. _____ _____

13. _____ _____

14. _____ _____

15. _____ _____

16. _____ _____

17. _____ _____

18. _____ _____

19. _____ _____

Lesson 19 Number Prefixes: **hemi**-, **semi**-, **uni**-, **bi**-, **tri**-

Say aloud each of the following words. Then, write each word on the lines provided.

Spelling Tip	Some prefixes express a specific number or quantity. The prefixes **hemi**- and **semi**- mean *half*. The prefix **uni**- means *one*. The prefix **bi**- means *two*. The prefix **tri**- means *three*.

Spelling Words

hemisphere _____

hemicycle _____

semiannual _____

semicircle _____

semifinal _____

unicorn _____

uniform _____

universe _____

biweekly _____

bicycle _____

bifocals _____

binoculars _____

biplane _____

triangle _____

tricycle _____

Lesson 19 Number Prefixes: **hemi**-, **semi**-, **uni**-, **bi**-, **tri**-

Words in Context

Complete the following journal entry with spelling words. One word is used twice.

September 13

Science class was interesting today. We are studying the

_____ and all of its planets and stars. I like learning about the
planets. The whole class seemed into it. Mr. Deibert had the class sit in a

_____, or as Mrs. Richards would say, "_____." He
set out different sizes of balls to represent the planets in relation to the Earth, sun,
and Moon.

After we finish this unit, we're going to study the Earth and the Western

_____ and the Eastern _____. I can't believe that
when it's summer in this hemisphere, it's winter in the other. I want to go there
when it's winter here so I can have summer all year long! Then, I could ride my

_____ on the trails without any snow.
This Saturday is our first soccer game. I'll pick up my new

_____ after school tomorrow. I like our colors: blue and yellow. I
think our team is going to be great this year. I'm sure we'll make it to the

_____ game again this year.
This Sunday, I'm gong on a hike with my dad. We're going to look for birds
and log them in a book. He says he has a present for me. I think it is a pair of

_____. I kept borrowing his on our last hike. I don't think he
minded, but it will be nice if we both have a pair to look at the far away birds.
Well, that's it for today. I have more math homework to do tonight. We're

studying shapes in geometry, like the _____ and the hexagon. It's
hard but kind of interesting. Better go!

Lesson 19   Number Prefixes: **hemi**-, **semi**-, **uni**-, **bi**-, **tri**-

Fun with Words
Match the prefixes on the left with the pictures on the right to make spelling words.

1. bi _____

5. bi _____

2. tri _____

6. uni _____

3. bi _____

7. hemi _____

4. semi _____

8. bi _____

Words Across the Curriculum
Write the science words on the lines beside each word.

1. biceps _____

3. triceps _____

2. quadriceps _____

Complete the following sentences with words from above.

1. The muscles in the body with three heads at the back

of the arm are called the _____.

2. Muscles with two heads at the front of the arm are

called the _____.

3. Large muscles in the lower body with four heads in the

front of the thighs are called the _____.

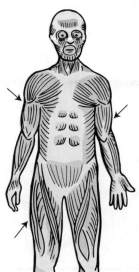

Lesson 19 Number Prefixes: **hemi-**, **semi-**, **uni-**, **bi-**, **tri-**

Words in Writing

Write two or three sentences about one of your favorite exercises or sports. Use at least three words from this lesson.

_____

_____

_____

Misspelled Words

Rewrite the misspelled spelling words correctly on the lines provided.

1. A hemicicle means the same thing as a semicircle. _____

2. If the doctor asks you to visit on a semianual basis, she wants to see you twice a year. _____

3. Some schools require students to wear a unform; so all of the students wear the same clothes. _____

4. If employees receive paychecks byweekly, they receive their checks once every two weeks. _____

5. A shape with three sides and three angles is a triangul. _____

6. The Earth can be divided into the Northern and Southern or the Western and Eastern Hemsphere. _____

7. Before the team plays in the championship, they must first win the simifinal. _____

8. A unihorn is a fictional animal with one long horn in the center of its forehead. _____

9. People who have a hard time seeing both near and far may need biphocals: eyeglasses that have lenses to help see both near and far. _____

10. A unicycle is a vehicle with one wheel; a bicycle is a vehicle with two wheels; a tricicle is a vehicle with three wheels. _____

Review Lessons 17–19

Write each of the following spelling words on the lines provided. Circle the prefixes **pre**- and **post**-.

1. prearrange _____

2. precaution _____

3. preheat _____

4. postdate _____

5. postpone _____

6. postwar _____

Complete the following letter with words from above.

Dear Aunt Dorothy,

    I just wanted to thank you for supporting my school fundraiser by participating in the auction. Thanks for letting me know that you

were going to _____ your check. That is not a problem, since the checks aren't due for another week.
    I think you will really like the weekend in the cabin. It was built in

the _____ era after World War II and it still has a lot of

its charm. The committee decided to _____ your plans so you don't have to worry about a thing. Just as a

_____, be sure to take plenty of sunscreen and bug spray, I don't want anything spoiling your weekend. Also, before you

cook anything, _____ the oven. You want to be sure it gets to the right temperature.

    Don't let rainy weather _____ your trip. The cabin has a sunroom, so you can kind of be inside and outside at the same time. I hope you and Uncle Roger have a wonderful time!

Thanks!

Diane

Review Lessons 17–19

Write the meaning of each prefix below.

1. im- _____

2. uni- _____

3. tri- _____

4. in- _____

5. hemi- _____

6. bi- _____

7. semi- _____

Write each of the following spelling words. Circle the prefixes.

1. imbalance _____

2. immeasurable _____

3. improper _____

4. inaccurate _____

5. indecisive _____

6. indirect _____

7. hemisphere _____

8. semiannual _____

9. universe _____

10. biweekly _____

11. binoculars _____

12. triangle _____

Unscramble the spelling words and write them on the lines provided.

1. There is an lanebimac _____ in strength between the two wrestlers.

2. Our seats were so far away, we had to use olarbcusni _____ to see the game.

3. The bill for dinner is curanitane _____ and is being corrected.

4. The student council meets wekeylib _____ in the meeting room.

5. The ways the volunteers helped at the bake sale were marsibelameu

_____.

6. The angles of a gnitarle _____ equal 180 degrees.

Lesson 20 Suffixes: -ate, -ive, -ship

Say each of the following words out loud. Then, write each word on the lines provided.

Spelling Tip	A **suffix** is a group of letters that is added to the end of a base word to change its meaning. The suffix -**ate** means *the state or quality of*. The suffix -**ive** means **inclined to**. The suffix -**ship** means *the state or quality of* or *the skill or art of*.

Spelling Words

activate   _____

constructive   _____

championship   _____

communicate   _____

creative   _____

friendship   _____

considerate   _____

effective   _____

hardship   _____

tortunate   _____

impressive   _____

leadership   _____

separate   _____

inventive   _____

relationship   _____

Lesson 20   Suffixes: -ate, -ive, -ship

Words in Context

Complete the following biography with spelling words. The first letter of each word has been given for you. Not all of the words are used. You will not repeat any of the words. Use a dictionary if you need help.

Martin Luther King, Jr.

One of America's greatest figures, Martin Luther King, Jr., born in Atlanta, Georgia, in 1929, is best known as one of America's greatest civil rights leaders.

In 1955, Martin Luther King, Jr. led the boycott of segregated bus lines in Montgomery, Alabama. The buses kept people of different

races s_____.

An i_____
victory followed in 1956 when Montgomery, Alabama, desegregated their busses. King's philosophy included nonviolent resistance. Such protests became

a c_____ method in gaining recognition of injustices and served to

a_____ thousands of people to march for justice. His

l_____ in civil rights and nonviolent resistance to end racial prejudice earned him the Nobel Peace Prize in 1964.

King's concerns also turned to those who faced one h_____ after another, such as the poor. Martin Luther King was assassinated in 1968.

Those who were f_____ enough to hear him speak knew he had a

c_____ and e_____ ability to c_____ to the public. King is considered a national hero and peacemaker.

Lesson 20 Suffixes: -ate, -ive, -ship

Fun with Words
Choose the correct spelling word that describes each illustration.

1. Our team is the victor. We won the _____!

2. I believe I'm connected to you somehow. I think we are

brothers. We have a _____.

3. The four of us are pals. Over the years, we have formed

a great _____.

4. I love to make and create things that did not exist before.

I am _____.

5. My teacher is kind and thoughtful. You could say she

is the most _____ person I know.

Words Across the Curriculum
Write the social studies words on the lines beside each word.

1. delicate _____

3. positive _____

2. negative _____

4. protective_____

Complete the following paragraph with words from above.

Endangered species are animals and plants whose existance are in danger due
to several different factors, such as chemical pollution and the loss of habitats.

However, the news is not completely _____. Some organizations are

having a _____ impact in helping endangered species. Wildlife

conservation groups are working to establish _____ habitats that stabilize

the _____ balance of life.

Lesson 20 Suffixes: -ate, -ive, -ship

Words in Writing

Write a biography about a historic figure. Use at least five words from this lesson.

_____

_____

_____

_____

_____

_____

_____

Using the Dictionary

Some words can serve as more than one part of speech, such as nouns, verbs, adjectives, or adverbs. The dictionary will tell you the different parts of speech (usually an abbreviation, such as **n** for _noun_) and provide the definition for each. Look up the following words in a dictionary. Write all of the parts of speech listed for each word.

1. activate _____

2. constructive _____

3. championship _____

4. communicate _____

5. creative _____

6. friendship _____

7. considerate _____

8. effective _____

9. hardship _____

10. fortunate _____

11. impressive _____

12. leadership _____

13. separate _____

14. inventive _____

15. relationship _____

16. delicate _____

17. negative _____

18. positive _____

19. protective _____

Lesson 21 Suffixes: -able, -ible

Say each of the following words out loud. Then, write each word on the lines provided.

Spelling Tip	The suffixes -**able** and -**ible** both mean *inclined to*.

Spelling Words

believable   _____

comfortable   _____

comparable   _____

memorable   _____

predictable   _____

reasonable   _____

reliable   _____

valuable   _____

washable   _____

convertible   _____

divisible   _____

invincible   _____

responsible   _____

sensible   _____

visible   _____

Lesson 21 Suffixes: -able, -ible

Words in Context

Complete the following paragraph with spelling words. The first letter of each word has been given for you. Not all of the words will be used. You will not use words more than once.

Mayan Pyramids

While they may not be c_____ to the famous Egyptian pyramids,

the pyramids of Mexico are just as m_____. The Maya is an ancient tribe
from southern Mexico and Central America. Their civilization formed around 1500 B.C.

The Mayas built seemingly i_____ pyramids. Some pyramids were built to
be climbed, with burial plots on top. Some were built to be sacred, without stairs, never
to be climbed. Many of them also served as observatories, as the Maya were
interested in the stars and planets.
        The city of Palenque was located in a dense rainforest. The pyramids and other

buildings there were built against a hill so they could be v_____ at great
distances through the forest. The city of Tikal is now located in the middle of a wildlife

preserve. This area of land is quite v_____ to the many birds and animals
that live there, some of which are endangered.

Mayans were a s_____ and organized people. Using mathematics,

solar eclipses were p_____. At the city of Uaxactún, the Maya built a

r_____ solar observatory that included a pyramid and three temples.
Mayan pyramids were impressive and functional. They reveal the intelligent and skilled
characteristics of the ancient Mayans.

Lesson 21 Suffixes: -able, -ible

Fun with Words

Convertibles come in different styles, colors, and sizes. One of the convertibles on this page can hold four passengers. The other convertible can hold three passengers. Make sure each car picks up the right number of passengers by answering the questions and writing the spelling words (the passengers) above the right car. The first one has been done for you.

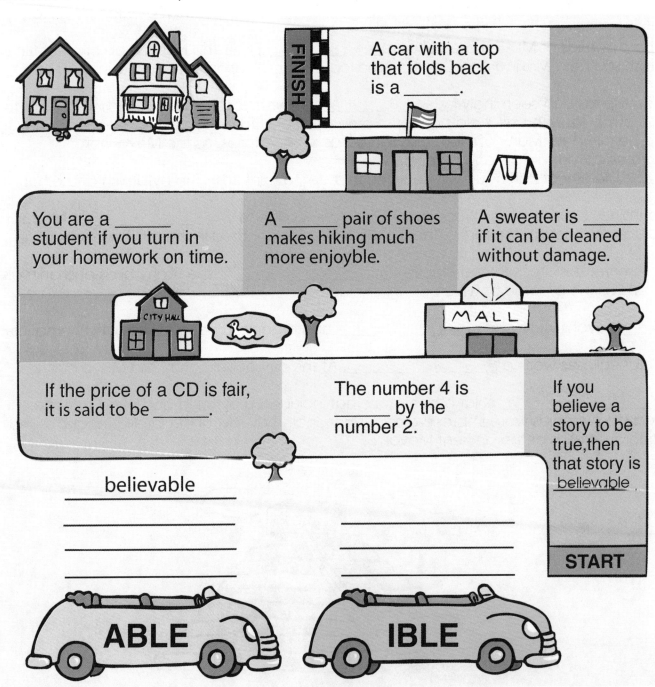

A car with a top that folds back is a _____.

You are a _____ student if you turn in your homework on time.

A _____ pair of shoes makes hiking much more enjoyble.

A sweater is _____ if it can be cleaned without damage.

If the price of a CD is fair, it is said to be _____.

The number 4 is _____ by the number 2.

If you believe a story to be true, then that story is believable.

START

believable
_____
_____
_____

ABLE

_____
_____

IBLE

Lesson 21 Suffixes: -able, -ible

Words in Writing

Create a game by writing questions using spelling words. The questions must be answered correctly in order for players to advance. Be creative and have fun!

_____

_____

_____

_____

_____

_____

_____

_____

Misspelled Words

The following narrative contains misspelled spelling words. Cross out the misspelled words and write them correctly above the misspelled word.

The sun was visable coming up over the mountain as the hikers started their day. The relyable guides had advised them to be sensable and pack comfortible shoes and clothing. The day was warm, so they brought plenty of water. The trail was hilly and the hikers were exhilarated by the vigorous exercise. It made them feel invinceble. Throughout the day, they saw unbelievable wildlife. They wrote in their journals about the foxes, coyotes, deer, and varied birds and squirrels they saw. Seeing animals in their own habitat made them feel responsable for taking care of the environment. By the end of the day they were exhausted but inspired. The day had not been predictible at all, with memorible surprises at every turn. The trip was a truly valueable experience.

Lesson 22 Suffixes: -ance, -ence, -ant, -ent

Say each of the following words out loud. Then, write each word on the lines provided.

Spelling Tip	The noun suffixes **-ance** and **-ence** both mean *the state or quality of.* The adjective suffixes **-ant** and **-ent** both mean *inclined to.*

Spelling Words

appearance   _____

distance   _____

entrance   _____

performance   _____

confidence   _____

excellence   _____

independence   _____

contestant   _____

hesitant   _____

Ignorant   _____

pleasant   _____

consistent   _____

intelligent   _____

persistent   _____

urgent   _____

Lesson 22 Suffixes: -ance, -ence, -ant, -ent

Words in Context

Complete the following passage with spelling words.

Jubilee!

Each _____ anxiouisly awaited the start of the quiz show. The three middle school students had been working all year for the opportunity to show off their skills.

This would be their first _____ on television. Each contestant knew that he

or she was _____, but there could only be one winner.

Their coaches had been _____ about what and how much the contestants studied. Rest was important, too. The coaches reminded them that some

contestants are _____ to the fact that starting a competition with a clear, rested mind can be just as vital as knowing the material.

Winning this competition could bring the winner some financial

_____. A college scholarship would be awarded to the winner. Thinking about that was really getting their stomachs tied in knots.

Finally, the sound of the host introducing the show could be heard back stage. The contestants' names were called. They wished each other luck and walked toward

the stage, ready to make their big _____.

Word Building

For the following nouns, write the words in their adjective forms. For the adjectives, write their noun forms. Use a dictionary if you need help. The first one has been done for you.

Nouns	Adjectives	Adjectives	Nouns
1. distance	distant	**1.** hesitant	_____
2. confidence	_____	**2.** ignorant	_____
3. excellence	_____	**3.** intelligent	_____
4. independence	_____	**4.** persistent	_____

Lesson 22 Suffixes: -ance, -ence, -ant, -ent

Fun with Words

Answer the questions for each contestant with spelling words.

Contestant #1

Contestant #2

Contestant #3

Question 1: noun: What is the length of a line between two points?

_____

Question 2: adjective: What is something that demands a quick action?

_____

Question 1: adjective: What else could an enjoyable day be called?

_____

Question 2: noun: What is the act of presenting, especially in front of an audience?

_____

Question 1: noun: What is something or someone that exhibits greatness?

_____

Question 2: adjective: What is something or someone that refuses to give up?

_____

Words Across the Curriculum

Write the science words on the lines beside each word.

1. accidents _____

2. coincidence _____

3. occurrences _____

4. sequence _____

The words above are scrambled in the following paragraph. Rewrite the words correctly.

A coincidence is a qucesene _____ of events that occur at the same time and that may or may not be connected. Mark Twain was born on the day that Halley's comet appeared. He died on the day that it reappeared. Harriet Tubman, a leader in the struggle against slavery, died on the same day that Rosa Parks, a leader in the Civil Rights Movement, was born. Are these and other

crencosucer _____ cenitacds _____? Some people

believe in random acts of cedoneicicn _____. Others believe that there is a reason for why everything happens. What do you believe?

Lesson 22 Suffixes: -ance, -ence, -ant, -ent

Words in Writing

Write a paragraph about a contest you have been in or a contest you have seen. Use at least five words from this lesson.

_____

_____

_____

_____

_____

_____

_____

_____

Using the Dictionary

Look up the following words in a dictionary. Rewrite the words and then write a brief definition of each word.

1. appearance _____ _____

2. contestant _____ _____

3. entrance _____ _____

4. ignorant _____ _____

5. independence _____ _____

6. intelligent _____ _____

7. occurrence _____ _____

8. sequence _____ _____

Review Lessons 20–22

Write each of the following spelling words on the lines provided. Circle the suffixes.

1. communicate _____

2. effective _____

3. predictable _____

4. valuable _____

5. performance _____

6. contestant _____

7. inventive _____

8. relationship _____

9. responsible _____

10. visible _____

11. persistent _____

12. excellence _____

Complete the following sentences with spelling words that have the suffixes -**ate**, -**ive**, and -**ship**. Then, answer the questions.

1. Having a good _____ with a pet is an enriching part of life.
Describe one that you have.

_____

2. What is your favorite way to _____: by telephone, letter, email, or face to face?

_____

3. Completing homework before dinner can be an _____ study habit.
Do you have a good study habit?

_____

4. Someone is _____ when they have a new idea or make something for the first time. Give an example how you have done this.

_____

Review Lessons 20-22

Complete the following sentences with spelling words that have the suffixes -**able** and -**ible** from page 108. Then, answer the questions.

1. The movie was _____; the audience knew the ending ten minutes after the movie began. What movie have you seen that had this same quality?

   _____

2. The lake was _____ from her kitchen window. What can you see

   from the windows in your classroom? _____

3. The daughter's bracelet was _____ because her father gave it to

   her. What means a lot to you? _____

4. The children and their parents were _____ for their new puppy. How have you shown that you are trustworthy and capable?

   _____

Complete the following sentences with spelling words that have the suffixes -**ance**, -**ence**, -**ant**, and -**ent** from page 108. Then, answer the questions.

1. A _____ takes part in a game or race. What is your favorite game or race?

   _____

2. If someone doesn't give up, then he or she is _____. Have you been this way?

   _____

3. What is your favorite _____: acting, singing, playing a musical instrument, or something else?

   _____

4. The winner of the vocabulary bee showed _____ in the subject. What is your favorite subject in school?

   _____

Lesson 23 Homophones

Say each of the following words out loud. Then, write each word on the lines provided.

Spelling Tip	**Homophones** are words that sound exactly the same but are spelled differently and have different meanings.

Spelling Words

leak _____

leek _____

canvas _____

canvass _____

patience _____

patients _____

presence _____

presents _____

sail _____

sale _____

scene _____

seen _____

their _____

there _____

they're _____

Lesson 23 Homophones

Words in Context

Complete the following sentences with the correct homophone form the spelling word list.

1. I bought two muffins and lemonade at the bake _____.

2. Using a _____ bag to grocery shop is good for the environment.

3. The doctor has many _____ to see.

4. Lynn and Leigh are sisters, and _____ best friends.

5. I think the faucet has a _____.

6. The actors rehearsed the same _____ for hours.

7. Haley and Hannah are playing soccer today. I'm going to go watch

   _____ game.

8. I love to go out on the lake and _____ in the summertime.

9. In order to be effective, teachers must have a lot of _____.

10. Have you _____ the play yet?

11. On Saturday, we plan to _____ the neighborhood to raise money for the tornado victims.

12. The oranges were left here and the bananas were left over _____.

13. How many _____ did you get for your birthday?

14. A _____, a vegetable in the onion family, would work well in that recipe.

15. Your _____ is required at the meeting.

Lesson 23 Homophones

Fun with Words

Each of the following pictures represents one of the homophones from the spelling word list. Identify each of the pictures by writing the homophone on the line provided.

1.

_____

3.

_____

5.

_____

2.

_____

4.

_____

Words Across the Curriculum

Write the science homophones on the lines beside each word.

1. tide _____   3. vane _____

2. tied _____   4. vein _____

Complete each of the following sentences with a homophone from above. Use a dictionary if you need help defining a word.

1. The weather _____ indicates a windy day ahead.

2. The _____ will be rolling in soon.

3. Let's make sure the boats are all _____ to the dock.

4. A _____ is a vessel that carries our blood.

Lesson 23 Homophones

Words in Writing

Write a paragraph about a piece of art you would like to create. Use four spelling words in your paragraph.

_____

_____

_____

_____

_____

_____

_____

_____

_____

_____

Misspelled Words

Cross out the misspelled word in each sentence and rewrite the word correctly.

1. The lek in the shower is driving me crazy. _____

2. The sails were made of a strong, heavy canvus. _____

3. The long training runs required a lot of pathients, but success at the track meet made it all worth it. _____

4. I'm going to add a leke to my salad. _____

5. The students were told to canves the area and hang up the bake sale fliers. _____

6. The pachents in the hospital were grateful for their visitors. _____

Lesson 24 Related Words

Say each of the following words out loud. Then, write each word on the lines provided.

Spelling Tip	Some pairings of words are related both in spelling and meaning.

Spelling Words

fact _____

factual _____

harmony _____

harmonious _____

human _____

humane _____

major _____

majority _____

muscle _____

muscular _____

nature _____

natural _____

produce _____

production _____

unite _____

unity _____

Lesson 24 Related Words

Words in Context

Complete the following paragraph with spelling words. Use a dictionary if you need help defining the words.

Living Together

The _____ is, as the world's population increases, the places that a

_____ being chooses to live moves more into the woods and forests.
These areas are homes to other creatures. Many different kinds of animals that live in

_____ and call these outlying areas home.
    As human beings push farther into the animals' habitats, the animals are moving
into areas populated by human beings. Is there any chance we can all live in

_____? It is up to the human beings to find a _____

balance for existence. Destroying the animals is not the answer. Some believe that is

not _____, and for the most part, it doesn't even solve the problem.

Eliminating some species upsets the _____ environmental balance.
Forcing some animals into extinction may eliminate the natural balance. Therefore,

some animals may become extinct while others _____ more.

    So, what are the answers to living in

_____? One _____
answer is through education. People are
becoming more educated on how to
coexist with wild animals. Human beings are
learning to respect and admire wild animals.
With work, it is possible for human beings and

animals to coexist and _____.

Lesson 24 Related Words

Fun with Words

Complete the following sentences by using the code and filling in the blanks with spelling words.

1=A	4=D	7=G	10=J	13=M	16=P	19=S	22=V	25=Y
2=B	5=E	8=H	11=K	14=N	17=Q	20=T	23=W	26=Z
3=C	6=F	9=I	12=L	15=O	18=R	21=U	24=X	

1. After the strenuous workout, my right calf ___ ___ ___ ___ ___ ___ was sore.
   13 21 19 3 12 5

2. The students read a ___ ___ ___ ___ ___ ___ ___ report that gave many statistics.
   6 I 3 20 21 I 12

3. The theater department is putting on a major

   ___ ___ ___ ___ ___ ___ ___ ___ ___ ___ in the spring.
   16 18 15 4 21 3 20 9 15 14

4. The ___ ___ ___ ___ ___ ___ ___ ___ of the students voted in
   13 I 10 15 18 9 20 25

   the election of the class president.

5. The horses were strong and ___ ___ ___ ___ ___ ___ ___ ___.
   13 21 19 3 21 12 I 18

Words Across the Curriculum

Write the language arts words on the lines beside each word.

1. poems _____   3. poetic _____

2. poetry _____

Complete the sentences with words from above.

1. The _____ in this book are some of my favorites.

2. _____ is one of my favorite topics to study in language arts.

3. Although not a poem, your letter sounded very _____.

NAME _____

Lesson 24 Related Words

Words in Writing

Write a poem about an animal of your choosing. Use at least three of the words from this lesson.

_____

_____

_____

_____

_____

Using the Dictionary

Use a dictionary to look up the differences between the following pairs of words. Rewrite the word, then write its part of speech (**n** for *noun* and **adj** for *adjective*) and a brief definition.

1. fact   word: _____   part of speech _____

      definition: _____

2. factual   word: _____   part of speech _____

      definition: _____

3. human   word: _____   part of speech _____

      definition: _____

4. humane   word: _____   part of speech _____

      definition: _____

5. muscle   word: _____   part of speech _____

      definition: _____

6. muscular   word: _____   part of speech _____

      definition: _____

Lesson 25 Latin and Greek Roots

Say each of the following words out loud. Then, write each word on the lines provided.

Spelling Tip	Most English words were created and developed from other languages. Many English words have Latin and Greek roots. Knowing what the roots mean can help you know what the English word means.

Spelling Words

autobiography   _____

autograph   _____

automatic   _____

megaphone   _____

microphone   _____

saxophone   _____

symphony   _____

telephone   _____

telecast   _____

telescope   _____

export   _____

import   _____

passport   _____

portable   _____

transport   _____

Lesson 25 Latin and Greek Roots

Words in Context

Each root has a specific meaning that gives us clues to the meanings of the words themselves.

Greek root: **auto**   meaning: *self or same*
Greek root: **phone**   meaning: *sound*
Greek root: **tele**   meaning: *distant*
Latin root: **port**   meaning: *to carry*

Complete the following sentences with spelling words.
Use the meanings of the roots to help you.

1. If one writes the story of one's own life, he or she is writing an _____.

2. This large cone-shaped tube, called a _____, sends a person's voice farther when one speaks into it.

3. A _____ sends a broadcast through air waves.

4. To carry goods out of one country to another is to _____ the goods.

5. When celebrities sign an _____, they are signing their own name.

6. An electronic device that magnifies sounds is called a _____.

7. Astronomers use a _____ to make distant objects seem closer.

8. To bring goods in from another country is to _____ the goods.

9. If something moves or works by itself, then it has an _____ operation.

10. A musical instrument that makes sound is a _____.

11. A _____ allows travelers to go in and out of other countries.

12. A _____ is a long piece of music for a full orchestra.

13. If something is easily carried it is said to be _____.

14. Trains, planes, and ships often carry, or _____, goods from one place to another.

15. _____ combines two Greek roots, one meaning *distant* and one meaning *sound*.

Lesson 25 Latin and Greek Roots

Fun with Words

Write each of the spelling words on the legs of the appropriate web. One word will go on two different webs.

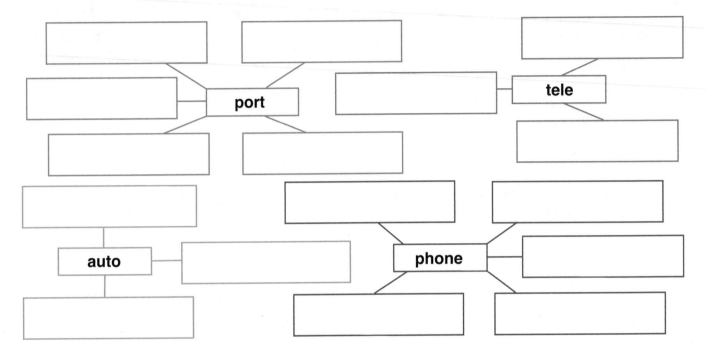

Words Across the Curriculum

Write the history words on the lines beside each word.

1. automobiles _____

3. telegraph _____

2. telegram _____

Complete each sentence with a history word.

1. It seems like most of the mail we receive today is electronic mail. But how did

people get mail before planes, trains, and _____?

2. The pony express operated in 1860 and 1861 between Missouri and California. The

_____, which sends messages by a code of electrical signals,
came into existence in 1861.

3. The _____ is the name of the messages that were sent by a system
of electrical signals.

Lesson 25 Latin and Greek Roots

Words in Writing

Choose two words from each of the Latin and Greek root groups: **auto**, **phone**, **tele**, and **port**. Write a short paragraph about an inventor you admire.

_____

_____

_____

_____

_____

_____

_____

Misspelled Words

The following dialogue contains misspelled spelling words. Cross out the incorrect words and write them correctly above the misspelled words.

The telefone rang and rang. It must have been important. On the last ring, Theo

burst through the door.

"Oh, no, I missed it," he groaned. He quickly dialed the number to get messages.

"Yes, it's from the symphoney...yes...yes...yes, I got in!" Theo was shouting

throughout the house, even though nobody else was home yet.

"What are you in?" asked Theo's dad as he walked through the back door.

"You're shouting so loud it sounds like you're screaming through a mecaphone."

"I'm the newest saxaphone player in the community junior symfhony," shouted Theo.

"Well, congratulations!" Theo's dad said as he gave him a big hug.

"You know being accepted isn't autematic, I practiced a lot," stated Theo.

"I know! Can I have your atograf now?" Theo's dad asked.

Lesson 26 Easily Confused Words

Say each of the following words out loud. Then, write each word on the lines provided.

Spelling Words

access _____

excess _____

choose _____

chose _____

finally _____

finely _____

later _____

latter _____

medal _____

metal _____

personal _____

personnel _____

recent _____

resent _____

sense _____

since _____

Lesson 26 Easily Confused Words

Words in Context
Complete the following sentences with spelling words.

1. Dylan has wanted to be a marine biologist _____ she was a little girl.

2. Do you think this road will give us _____ to the park?

3. Between pizza and pasta, Mitzi prefers the _____.

4. The person in charge of hiring is called the _____ director.

5. Can we _____ two or three side dishes to go along with the entrée?

6. The _____ storms left the town without electricity for two days.

7. _____, the rain ended, and we could finish the baseball game.

8. If you eat the whole pizza you will definitely be eating to _____.

9. The art sculpture was made of _____.

10. Does it make _____ to start the project now?

11. After we have eaten, let's go to the _____ showing of the movie.

12. Greg _____ to work on his history homework before his math.

13. Louis won the first place _____ in the science fair.

14. Leigh _____ the fax when it didn't appear to go through the first time.

15. The chef _____ chopped the vegetables.

Word Building
The prefix **re-** means *again* or *back*. The suffix **-ly** means *having the attribute of*. Add the prefix to the first word and the suffix to the second word. Then, write the definition for new each word.

1. appear _____   _____

2. scholar _____   _____

Lesson 26 Easily Confused Words

Fun with Words

Find and circle each spelling word in the puzzle below. They can be horizontal, vertical, forward, backward, or diagonal. Once you have found them, write them on the lines next to the puzzle.

1. _____

2. _____

3. _____

4. _____

5. _____

6. _____

7. _____

8. _____

9. _____

10. _____

11. _____

12. _____

13. _____

14. _____

15. _____

16. _____

e	x	c	e	s	s	m	u	n	r
c	m	h	k	i	n	s	c	o	e
p	e	r	s	o	n	a	l	o	s
t	t	e	r	w	a	c	r	d	e
l	a	d	e	m	w	c	e	e	n
b	l	b	y	b	r	e	u	s	t
n	g	e	e	b	s	u	n	z
z	g	r	t	e	g	s	e	e	j
u	d	a	y	f	r	c	e	s	d
m	l	a	r	j	e	o	r	s	i
e	a	e	a	r	k	k	o	i	n
y	t	a	n	c	c	o	c	n	l
l	t	u	m	n	b	h	u	c	s
l	e	m	a	r	o	a	o	e	t
a	r	h	o	o	n	s	s	s	t
n	n	t	s	j	i	m	r	c	e
i	a	e	h	s	m	r	s	e	l
f	i	n	e	l	y	h	s	z	p

Lesson 26 Easily Confused Words

Words in Writing
Write about a time when you exercised too long or stayed up too late. How did you feel afterward? Would you do this same thing again?

_____

_____

_____

_____

_____

_____

_____

Using the Dictionary
Use a dictionary to look up the definitions of the following pairs of words. Rewrite each word and then write a brief definition for each.

1. access: _____ _____

2. excess: _____ _____

3. later: _____ _____

4. latter: _____ _____

5. medal: _____ _____

6. metal: _____ _____

7. recent: _____ _____

8. resent: _____ _____

9. sense: _____ _____

10. since: _____ _____

Lesson 27 Using a Dictionary and Thesaurus

Dictionaries are useful in many ways. Not only can you learn how to spell a word, but you can also learn the origin of the word, its part of speech, and definitions, as well as any alternate spellings. Words are listed alphabetically. The word you are looking up in a dictionary is called the **entry word**.

When you are looking up your entry word, go to the first letter of your word. For example, if you are looking up *proton*, go to the letter **p** first. From there, you can use guide words to help you narrow down the page. **Guide words** are located at the top of each page. The first guide word is the first word on the page. The second guide word is the last word on the page.

prosthetics to proud

pros•thet•ics (pros thet'iks) n. surgery or dentistry that deals with artificial structures. **2.** the fa

If the word you are looking up is between the guide words alphabetically, then the word is on that page.

Once you have found your entry word on the page, there is a wealth of information about the word. After the entry word, you will see its pronunciation. The pronunciation will help you to pronounce the word if you are unsure. If you are unclear about some of the pronunciation marks used, find the pronunciation key in the dictionary.

unit or cell. 2. a person or thing that is formed first; original; prototype. 3. the hypothetical first individual or species.

pro•to•type (prō'tə tīp), n. v. 1. the original or model on which som

After the pronunciation will be the entry word's part of speech, usually abbreviated, **n.** for *noun*, **v.** for *verb*, **adj.** for *adjective*, or **adv.** for *adverb*. Sometimes, a word has more than one part of speech. All of the parts of speech will be given for an entry word.

The definition of the entry word for each part of speech will be given after the abbreviation of the part of speech. Sometimes more than one definition exists. Each definition will be listed with numbers. Sometimes, example sentences are given along with the definition to help clarify that particular definition.

pro•to•type (prō' tə tīp), n., v. -n **1.** the original or model on which something is based or formed; pattern. **2.** someone that serves as a typical example. -v **3.** to create a prototype.

Lesson 27 Using a Dictionary and Thesaurus

In addition to the various parts of speech of the entry word, plurals of nouns, tenses of verbs, and comparatives and superlatives of adjectives will also be noted.

Sometimes, even a picture will be given to help illustrate an entry word.

A **thesaurus** is also a valuable reference tool, providing synonyms and antonyms for the entry word.

A thesaurus is set up just like a dictionary, with each entry word listed alphabetically and guide words at the top of each page. Each entry word will list its part of speech and then synonyms for that word. Some thesauruses will even have sample sentences using the entry word. There will also be a list of antonyms for the entry word.

A thesaurus is particularly useful when writing. Using synonyms and antonyms will make writing more lively with more variety.

Place these words in alphabetical order. Then, look them up in the dictionary. Write each word, their pronunciations, parts of speech, and definitions on the lines provided. If a word has more than one part of speech, write the part of speech and definition for the first listed.

animal	audience	teamwork	harmony	telescope
historical	compassion	postscript	cartoon	medal

1. word _____   pronunciation _____

 part of speech _____   definition _____

 _____

2. word _____   pronunciation _____

 part of speech _____   definition _____

 _____

3. word _____   pronunciation _____

 part of speech _____   definition _____

 _____

Lesson 10 Using a Dictionary and Thesaurus

4. word _____   pronunciation _____

     part of speech _____   definition _____

_____

5. word _____   pronunciation _____

     part of speech _____   definition _____

_____

6. word _____   pronunciation _____

     part of speech _____   definition _____

_____

7. word _____   pronunciation _____

     part of speech _____   definition _____

_____

8. word _____   pronunciation _____

     part of speech _____   definition _____

_____

9. word _____   pronunciation _____

     part of speech _____   definition _____

_____

10. word _____   pronunciation _____

     part of speech _____   definition _____

_____

Lesson 10 Using a Dictionary and Thesaurus

Look up the following words in a thesaurus. Write one synonym and one antonym (if one is given) for each word. Then, write a sentence using the synonym in one sentence and the antonym in another.

1. athletic   synonym _____   antonym _____

synonym sentence   _____

antonym sentence   _____

2. friendship   synonym _____   antonym _____

synonym sentence   _____

antonym sentence   _____

3. informal   synonym _____   antonym _____

synonym sentence   _____

antonym sentence   _____

4. memorable   synonym _____   antonym _____

synonym sentence   _____

antonym sentence   _____

5. scenic   synonym _____   antonym _____

synonym sentence   _____

antonym sentence   _____

6. visible   synonym _____   antonym _____

synonym sentence   _____

antonym sentence   _____

Review Lessons 23–27

Write each of the following spelling words on the lines provided.

1. leak _____

2. leek _____

3. presence _____

4. presents _____

5. fact _____

6. factual _____

7. nature _____

8. natural _____

9. unite _____

10. unity _____

Choose five spelling words from above and write them in alphabetical order. Then, use a dictionary to write their pronunciations, parts of speech, and definitions.

1. word _____   pronunciation _____

  part of speech _____   definition _____

  _____

2. word _____   pronunciation _____

  part of speech _____   definition _____

  _____

3. word _____   pronunciation _____

  part of speech _____   definition _____

  _____

4. word _____   pronunciation _____

  part of speech _____   definition _____

  _____

5. word _____   pronunciation _____

  part of speech _____   definition _____

LESSONS 23–27 REVIEW

Spectrum Spelling
Grade 6
130

Review
Lessons 23–27

Review Lessons 23–27

Write each of the following spelling words on the lines provided.

1. autograph _____

2. automatic _____

3. portable _____

4. transport _____

5. finely _____

6. later _____

7. latter _____

8. medal _____

9. personal _____

10. recent _____

Choose seven spelling words from above and write them in alphabetical order. Then, look them up in a thesaurus and write one synonym and one antonym for each.

1. word _____

antonym _____

synonym _____

2. word _____

antonym _____

synonym _____

3. word _____

antonym _____

synonym _____

4. word _____

antonym _____

synonym _____

5. word _____

antonym _____

synonym _____

6. word _____

antonym _____

synonym _____

7. word _____

antonym _____

synonym _____

LESSONS 23–27 REVIEW

A

ac·cess *n.* Admission, entrance; permission or power to enter. ak′ ses

ac·ci·dents *pl. n.* Unplanned or unexpected events. ak′ si dents

ac·com·plish·ment *n.* A finished task; completion of effort, especially admirable or noteworthy. ə käm′ plish mənt

a·chieve *v.* To set or reach by trying hard; to succeed in doing. ə chēv′

ac·ti·vate *v.* To put into action; to begin or make active. ak′ ti vāt

ad·dress *v.* To direct or aim; to speak to; to give attention to. *n.* The location to which mail or goods can be sent to a person. ə dres′

af·ford *v.* To be able to provide; to have enough money to spare. ə fôrd′

air·planes *pl. n.* Fixed-wing vehicles capable of flight. er′ plānz

al·pha·bet *n.* The letters of a language, arranged in an order fixed by custom. al′ fə bet

an·cient *adj.* Very old; from a time long past; belonging to the early history of people. *n.* An extremely elderly person in a position of wisdom or authority. ān′ chənt

an·i·mal *n.* Any being other than a human being; any four-footed creature; beast. an′ ə məl

an·nounce·ment *n.* A public statement. ə nouns′ mənt

ap·pear·ance *n.* The action or process of appearing; an outward indication or showing. ə pir′ əns

ap·point·ment *n.* The act of appointing or designating; arrangement for or time of a meeting. ə point′ mənt

as·cend *v.* To rise up from a lower level; to climb; to mount; to walk up. ə send′

ath·let·ic *adj.* Physically strong and active. ath let′ ik

at·ti·tude *n.* A mental position; a predisposition or assumption at the start of a communication. at′ ə tüd

au·di·ence *n.* A group of listeners; those in attendance at an event or performance. ô′ dē əns

au·di·to·ri·um *n.* A large room in a public building or a school that holds many people. ô də tôr′ ē əm

au·to·bi·og·ra·phy *n.* The life story of a person, written by that person. ôt ō bī äg′ rə fē

au·to·graph *n.* A handwritten signature. *v.* To sign with one's signature. ôt′ ə graf

au·to·mat·ic *adj.* Operating with little control; without thought or premeditation. ôt ə mat′ ik

au·to·mo·biles *pl. n.* Four-wheeled passenger vehicles commonly propelled by an internal combustion engine; cars. ôt′ ə mə bēlz

au·tumn *n.* The season between summer and winter; the fall. ôt′ əm

a·void *v.* To stay away from; to shun; to prevent or keep from happening. ə void′

awk·ward *adj.* Lacking grace or felicity; clumsy. ôk′ wərd

awn·ing *n.* Roof-like structure, often of canvas, that serves as a shelter over a window. ôn′ ing

B

back·yard *n.* An area to the rear of a house for recreation or storage. bak yärd′

bass *n.* A musical instrument. bās

bat·tle *n.* A struggle; combat between opposing forces. bat′ l

bea·vers *pl. n.* Large semiaquatic rodents with webbed feet and flat tails. bē′ vərz

be·hav·ior *n.* How someone acts. bē hāv′ yər

be·liev·a·ble *adj.* Able to be believed; trustworthy. bē lēv′ ə bəl

be·low *adv.* At a lower level or place. bē lō′

bi·ceps *pl. n.* Large muscles in the front of the upper arm and at the back of the thigh. bī seps

bi·cy·cle *n.* A two-wheeled vehicle propelled by pedals, designed for one rider. bī′ si kəl

bi·fo·cals *n.* Glasses to correct both close and distant vision. bī′ fō kəlz

bin·oc·u·lars *pl. n.* An optical magnifying device for both eyes at once. bi näk′ yə lərz

bi·plane *n.* A glider or airplane with wings on two levels. bī′ plān

bird·bath *n.* A shallow basin of water set out for birds. burd′ bath

bi·week·ly *n.* Occurring every two weeks. bī wēk′ lē

blue *n.* A color the same as the color of a clear daytime sky. *adj.* feeling sad. blü

bod·y *n.* The physical part of a person; the main part of a written piece. bäd′ ē

book·shel·ves *pl. n.* Open shelving areas used to display and store books. book′ shelvz

bot·tle *n.* A container with a narrow neck and a top that can be closed. bät′ l

boy·cott *v.* To abstain from dealing with, buying, or using. boi′ kät

bright *adj.* Brilliant in color or light; vivid; shining and emitting or reflecting light. brīt

broad *adj.* Covering a wide area. brôd

broc·co·li *n.* A green vegetable from the cauliflower family. bräk′ ə lē

bu·reau *n.* A branch of the government; a low chest for storing clothes. byū′ rō

but·ter·fly *n.* A flying insect with four broad, colorful wings. but′ ər flī

C

calves *pl. n.* Young offspring of the domestic cow. kavz

cam·el *n.* A large mammal used in desert regions as transportation. kam′ əl

can·vas *n.* A heavy fabric used in making tents and for oil paintings. kan′ vəs

can·vass *v.* To travel through a region to solicit opinions or votes. kan′ vəs

can·yon *n.* A deep and narrow gorge with steep sides. kan′ yən

car·toon *n.* A humorous, illustrated story in one or several panels; a comic strip. kär tün′

cas·tle *n.* A fort or fortified dwelling for nobility. kas′ əl

chain *n.* A connection of several links, usually made of metal. chān

cham·pi·on *n.* The holder of first place in a contest. cham′ pē ən

cham·pi·on·ship *n.* The competition that determines a winner. cham′ pē ən ship

check *v.* To control or restrain; to review for accuracy. *n.* A written order for a bank to pay that amount of money. chek

child·ren *pl. n.* More than one child. chil′ drən

chim·pan·zee *n.* An ape with large ears and dark brown hair. chim pan′ zē

choc·o·late *n.* A mixture of ground and roasted cacao nuts, usually sweetened. chôk′ ə lət

choice *n.* The act of selection. chois

choose *v.* To select or pick out. chüz

chose *v.* Selected or picked out. chōz

cit·ies *pl. n.* Self-governed permanently located communities of residences and businesses. sit′ ēz

class·mate *n.* A member of one's class. klas′ māt

class·room *n.* A room in a school building where lessons are taught. klas′ rüm

clean *adj.* Free from impurities, dirt, or contamination; neat in habits. klēn

cloud *n.* A visible body of water or ice particles floating in the atmosphere. kloud

clum·sy *adj.* Lacking coordination, grace, or dexterity; not tactful or skillful. klum′ zē

clus·ters *pl. n.* Bunches; bouquets; groups or gatherings. klus′ tərz

coach *n.* A trainer or director of athletics. kōch

coast *n.* The land bordering the sea. *v.* To slide or glide along. kōst

cod *n.* A large fish of the North Atlantic. käd

coil *n.* A series of connecting rings. *v.* To retract into a striking position. koil

coin *n.* A flat, rounded piece of metal used as money. koin

co·in·ci·dence *n.* Two events happening at the same time by accident but appearing to have some connection. kō in′ si dəns

col·lege *n.* An school of higher education that grants a bachelor's degree. käl′ ij

col·umn *n.* A supporting pillar used in construction; a vertical division of typed or printed lines on paper. käl′ əm

com·e·dy *n.* A humorous, entertaining performance with a happy ending. käm′ ə dē

com·fort·a·ble *adj.* In a state of comfort. kum′ fər tə bəl

com·mer·cial *n.* An advertisement on radio or television. kə mur′ shəl

com·mit·tee *n.* A group of persons appointed or elected to perform a particular task or function. kə mit′ ē

com·mu·ni·cate *v.* To transmit information, to share information. kə myün′ ni kāt

com·mu·ni·ty *n.* A group of people living in the same area and under the same government. kə myü′ ni tē

com·pa·ra·ble *adj.* Capable of comparison; worthy of comparison; similar. käm′ pər ə bəl

com·pas·sion *n.* Deep, sincere, and longstanding sympathy for someone suffering or distressed. kəm pash′ ən

con·do·min·i·um *n.* An apartment in which all units are owned separately. kän də min′ ē əm

con·fi·dence *n.* A feeling of self-assurance; a feeling of trust in a person; reliance. kän′ fi dəns

con·sid·er·ate *adj.* Having care for other's feelings. kən sid′ ər ət

con·sis·tent *adj.* Being steady; predictable. kən sis′ tənt

con·struc·tive *adj.* Useful; helpful; not destructive. kən struk′ tiv

con·tes·tant *n.* One who participates in a contest. kən tes′ tənt

con·vert·i·ble *n.* A car with a top that folds back or can be removed completely. kən vurt′ i bəl

cos·tume *n.* Clothes worn by a person playing a part or dressing up in disguise. käs′ tōōm

could've *contr.* Short form of could have. kood′ əv

cre·a·tive *adj.* Marked by the ability to create. krē ā′ tiv

crowd *n.* A large group of people gathered together. kroud

D

da·ta·bases *pl. n.* Places where computers store information for ease of use. dāt′ ə bās əs or dat′ ə bās əs

daz·zle *v.* To amaze or invoke wonder. daz′ əl

debt *n.* The money or promise someone owes to someone else. det

del·i·cate *adj.* Pleasing in color, taste, or aroma; made finely and carefully; fragile. del′ i kət

de·part·ment *n.* The division or part of a company, college, or store. di pärt′ mənt

de·ter·mine *v.* To settle or decide by the facts; to figure out. di tur′ mən

dic·tion·ar·ies *pl. n.* Reference books containing alphabetically arranged words together with their definitions and usages. dik′ shə ner ēz

di·lem·ma *n.* A predicament requiring a choice between equally undesirable alternatives. di lem′ ə

di·rec·tor *n.* A person who manages or directs. də rek′ tər

dis·cov·er·ies *pl. n.* Items or ideas found. di skuv′ ər ēz

dis·play *v.* To show or put on exhibit; to give a demonstration of. *n.* An object used to show information. di splā′

dis·tance *n.* The measure between two points. dis′ təns

dis·tri·bu·tion *n.* The act of giving something out. dis tri byū′ shən

dis·turb *v.* To destroy the balance or rest; to unsettle; to bother. di sturb′

di·vis·i·ble *adj.* Able to be divided into smaller parts. də viz′ ə bəl

doesn't *contr.* Short form of *does not.* duz′ ənt

dom·i·noes *pl. n.* Small rectangular blocks of wood or plastic with faces marked with dots. däm′ ə nōz

don't *contr.* Short form of *do not.* dōnt

doubt *v.* To be uncertain about something; to distrust. dout

drew *v.* Sketched. drü

E

ea·gles *pl. n.* Large birds of prey. ē′ gəlz

ea·sel *n.* A frame used by artists to support a canvas or picture. ē′ zəl

ef·fec·tive *adj.* Producing an expected effect or proper result. ə fək′ tiv

ef·fi·cient *adj.* Adequate in performance with a minimum of waste or effort. ə fish′ ənt

em·pa·thy *n.* Identification with and understanding the feelings of another person. em′ pə thē

em·ploy *v.* To engage the service or use of; to hire; to use. em ploi′

en·joy *v.* To feel joy or find pleasure in something. en joi′

en·trance *n.* The act of entering; the means or place of entry. en′ trəns

es·cape *v.* To break free from capture or restraint. e skāp

es·pe·cial·ly *adv.* Having a larger degree of mention or need. e spesh′ əl ē

eve·ry·bo·dy *pron.* Every person. ev′ rē bäd ē

eve·ry·one *pron.* Everybody; every person. ev′ rē wun

eve·ry·where *adv.* In, at, or to every place; in all places. ev′ rē hwer

ev·i·dence *n.* Signs or facts on which a conclusion can be based. ev′ ə dəns

ex·am·ple *n.* A representative as a sample; a problem or exercise in arithmetic to show a rule or practice. eg zam′ pəl

ex·ca·va·tion *n.* Act of digging holes in search of somthing. eks kə vā′ shənz

ex·cel·lence *n.* The state or quality of being superior or outstanding. ek′ sə ləns

ex·cel·lent *adj.* Being superior or outstanding. ek′ sə lənt

ex·cept *prep.* With the omission or exclusion of. ek sept′

ex·cep·tion·al *adj.* Being an exception to the rule; well above average; outstanding. ek sep′ shən əl

ex·cess *n.* The condition of going beyond what is necessary, usual, or proper. ek′ ses

ex·port *v.* To carry or send merchandise or raw materials to other countries for resale or trade. eks′ spôrt

F

fact *n.* Something that actually occurred or exists. fakt

fac·tu·al *adj.* Containing or consisting of facts, literal and exact. fak′ chü əl

fan·tas·tic *adj.* Superb. fan tas′ tik

fas·ci·nate *v.* To attract irresistibly. fas′ ə nāt

fer·ries *pl. n.* Boats or other crafts used to transport people and vehicles across a body of water. fer′ ēz

fi·nal·ly *adv.* Happening at the end. fī′ nəl lē

fine·ly *adv.* To a small point. fīn′ lē

fin·ish *v.* To bring to or reach an end; to conclude. fin′ ish

first *adj.* Preceding all others. furst

fla·min·gos *pl. n.* Large, long-necked, tropical wading birds, having very long legs, and pink or red plumage. flə ming′ gōz

for·tu·nate *adj.* Brought about by good fortune; having good fortune. fôr′ chə nət

frac·tion *n.* A small part; in mathematics, an indicated quantity less than a whole number. frak′ shən

freight *n.* A service of transporting commodities by air, land or water. frāt

friend·ship *n.* The state of being friends. frend′ ship

G

geese *pl. n.* Large water birds related to swans and ducks. gēs

gla·cier *n.* A large mass of compacted snow that moves slowly. glā′ shər

grand *adj.* To be large in size, extent, or scope. grand

great *adj.* Very large in size or volume. grāt

growth *n.* The act or process of growing. grōth

guard·i·an *n.* One assigned responsibility for the care of a person or property. gär′ dē ən

guid·ance *n.* The act, process, or result of guiding. gīd′ ns

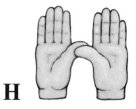

H

hall·way *n.* A corridor. hôl′ wā

hard·ship *n.* A painful, difficult condition. härd′ ship

har·mo·ni·ous *adj.* Being in complete agreement. Presenting a pleasing sound. här mō′ nē əs

har·mo·ny *n.* Complete agreement, as of feeling or opinion. A pleasing sound. här′ mə nē

hasn't *contr.* Short form of *has not.* haz′ ənt

he'd contr. Short form of *he had.* hēd

hem·i·cy·cle *n.* A semicircle. hem′ i sī kəl

hem·i·sphere *n.* A half sphere divided by a plane passing through its center. hem′ i sfir

hes·i·tant *adj.* Given to hesitating; lacking decisiveness. hez′ i tənt

his·tor·ic *adj.* Significant or famous in history. his tôr′ ik

hi·stor·i·cal *adj.* Relating to or taking place in history. his tôr′ i kəl

home·room *n.* A room where a group of students meet everyday. hōm′ rüm

house *n.* A building that serves as living quarters for one or more families; home. hous

hu·man *adj.* Having or manifesting human form or attributes. hyū′ mən

hu·mane *adj.* To be marked by compassion, sympathy, or consideration for other people or animals. hyū mān′

hu·mid *adj.* Containing a large amount of moisture; damp. hyū′ mid

hum·ming·bird *n.* A very small bird with narrow wings, a slender bill, and a very long tongue. hum′ ing burd

hu·mor·ous *adj.* Full of humor and laughter. Funny. hyū′ mər əs

hun·dred *n.* The number after ninety-nine and before one hundred and one. hun′ drəd

hus·band *n.* A man who is married. huz′ bənd

I

i·den·ti·cal *adj.* Being the same; exactly equal or much alike. ī den′ ti kəl

ig·no·rant *adj.* Lacking education or knowledge; not aware. ig′ nər ənt

im·bal·ance *n.* A lack of functional balance; defective coordination. im bal′ əns

im·ma·ture *adj.* Not fully grown; undeveloped; suggesting a lack of maturity. im ə choor′

im·meas·ur·a·ble *adj.* Not capable of being measured. im mezh′ ər ə bəl

im·mersed *adj.* Put completely underwater. im murst′

im·mo·bi·lize *v.* To render motionless, preventing movement. im mō′ bə līz

im·mu·ni·za·tion *n.* To provide immunity to a disease through medicine. im myū nə zā′ shən

im·per·fect *adj.* Not perfect. im pur′ fikt

im·po·lite *adj.* Rude; without courtesy. im pə līt′

im·port *v.* To bring in goods from a foreign country for trade or sale. im′ pôrt

im·pos·si·ble *adj.* Not capable of existing or happening. im päs′ ə bəl

im·pres·sive *adj.* Making a strong impression; striking. im pres′ iv

im·prop·er *adj.* Unsuitable; incorrect. im präp′ ər

in·ac·cu·ra·te *adj.* Incorrect. in ak′ yər ət

in·ac·tive *adj.* Not active or inclined to be active; out of current use or service. in ak′ tiv

in·ca·pa·ble *adj.* Lacking the ability for doing or performing. in kā′ pə bəl

in·con·sid·er·ate *adj.* Not considerate; thoughtless. in kən sid′ ər ət

in·de·ci·sive *adj.* Without a clear-cut result; marked by indecision. in di sī′ siv

in·de·pend·ence *n.* The quality or state of being independent. in di pen′ dəns

in·di·rect *adj.* Not taking a direct course; not straight to the point. in də rekt′

in·ex·pen·sive *adj.* Not expensive. in ek spen′ siv

in·fect·ed *v.* Contaminated with disease-causing microorganisms; transmited a disease to. in fek′ td

in·fec·tion *n.* Invasion of a bodily part by disease-causing microorganisms. in fek′ shən

in·flu·en·tial *adj.* Having influence or say over others. in flü en′ shəl

in·for·mal *adj.* Not formal. in fôr′ məl

in·for·ma·tion *n.* Knowledge gained from study or discussion. in fər mā′ shən

in·hale *v.* To breathe or draw into the lungs. in hāl′

in·no·va·tion *n.* Something new. in ə vā′ shən

in·spi·ra·tion *n.* The stimulation within the mind of some idea, feeling, or impulse which leads to creative action. in spər ā′ shən

in·stall *v.* To put in position for service; to place into an office or position. in stôl′

in·tel·li·gent *adj.* Having or showing intelligence. in tel′ ə jənt

in·trigue *v.* To arouse the curiosity or interest; to fascinate. in′ trēg

in·tro·duc·tion *n.* A passage of a book that will introduce the story or the content of a book; something which introduces. in trə duk′ shən

in·ven·tive *adj.* Being able to create or invent. in ven′ tiv

in·vin·ci·ble *adj.* Unable to be hurt or defeated. in vin′ sə bəl

it's *contr.* Short form of *it is* and *it has.* its

J

joint *n.* The place where two or more things or parts are joined. joint

K

kick·ing *v.* Striking something with force by the foot. kik′ ing

L

la·bel *n.* Something that identifies or describes. v. To attach a label to. lā′ bəl

lakes *pl. n.* Large, inland bodies of either salt or fresh water. lāks

lan·gua·ges *n.* Words, sounds, pronunciations, and methods of combining words used and understood by people. lang′ gwij əs

larg·er *adj.* Greater in amount or size than others. lärj′ ər

lat·er *adj.* Coming after others. lāt′ ər

lat·ter *adj.* Being the second of two things. lat′ ər

lead·er·ship *n.* The ability to guide or lead. lēd′ ər ship

league *n.* An association of persons, organizations, or states for common interest. lēg

leak *n.* An opening, as a flaw or small crack, permitting an escape or entrance of light or fluid. lēk

leek *n.* An edible herb related to the onion. lēk

let's *contr.* Short form of let us. lets

let·ters *pl. n.* Standard characters used in writing or printing; written or printed means of communication sent to another person. let′ ərz

lev·el *n.* A standard position from which other heights and depths are measured. adj. Balanced in height; even. v. To make or become flat. lev′ əl

li·brar·ies *pl. n.* Collections of books, pamphlets, magazines, and reference books kept for reading, reference, or borrowing; buildings that lend books. lī′ brer ēz

M

main·tain *v.* To carry on or to keep in existence. mān tān′

ma·jor *adj.* Greater in importance, quantity, number, or rank. mā′ jər

ma·jor·i·ty *n.* The greater number of something; more than half. mə jôr′ ə tē

mar·a·thon *n.* A foot race of slightly more than 26 miles, usually run on the streets of a city. mer′ ə thän

mead·ow *n.* A tract of grassland used for grazing or growing hay. me dō′

med·al *n.* A small piece of metal presented as an award. med′ əl

med·i·a *pl. n.* The instruments of news communication, as radio, television, and newspapers. mē′ dē ə

meg·a·phone *n.* A cone-shaped object used to project a voice or sound. meg′ ə fōn

mem·o·ra·ble *adj.* Worth remembering or noting. mem′ ər ə bəl

men *pl. n.* More than one man. men

men·tion *v.* To refer to incidentally, in passing, or briefly. men′ shən

met·al *n.* An element that produces a durable structure, such as steel and iron. met′ l

meth·od *n.* A manner, a process, or the regular way of doing something. meth′ əd

mice *pl. n.* More than one mouse. mīs

mi·cro·phone *n.* An instrument that converts acoustical waves into electrical signals and feeds them into a recorder or amplifier. mī′ krə fōn

mi·grate *v.* To move from one place to another or from one climate to another. mī′ grāt

min·er·al *n.* A solid substance, such as silver, diamond, or quartz, that is taken from the earth. min′ ər əl

mir·ror *n.* A surface of glass that reflects light, forming the image of an object. mir′ ər

mod·ern *adj.* Typical of the recent past or the present; advanced or up-to-date. mäd′ ərn

mole *n.* A small, burrowing mammal. mōl

moose *n.* A large, northern mammal, similar to a deer. müs

moun·tain *n.* A land mass that rises above its surroundings and is higher than a hill. mount′ n

mus·cle *n.* Bodily tissue that consists of long cells that contract when stimulated. mus′ əl

mus·cu·lar *adj.* Having large muscles. mus′ kyū lər

must·n't *contr.* Short from of *must not.* mus′ ənt

na·tion *n.* A group of people under one government. nā′ shən

nat·u·ral *adj.* Produced or existing by nature. nach′ ər əl

na·ture *n.* The universe and its phenomena. nā′ chər

nec·es·sar·y *adj.* Unavoidable; required; essential; needed. nes′ ə ser ē

neg·a·tive *adj.* Expressing denial or disapproval; not positive. neg′ ə tiv

news·pa·per *n.* A weekly or daily publication that contains recent information. nüz′ pā pər

nick·el *n.* A U.S. coin worth five cents. nik′ əl

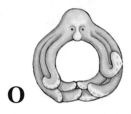

oc·cu·pa·tion *n.* A job, profession, or vocation. äk yū pā′ shən

oc·cur·ren·ces *pl. n.* Events happening. ə kur′ əns əs

of·fi·cer *n.* A person who holds a title, position, or office. ôf′ i sər

of·fi·cial *adj.* Something derived from proper authority. *n.* One who holds a position or office. ə fish′ əl

o·rig·i·nal *adj.* Belonging to the first or beginning. n. A new idea produced by one's own imagination. ə rij′ ə nəl

out·side *n.* The area beyond the boundary lines or surface; an area not inside. out sīd′

ox·en *pl. n.* Animals used domestically in much the same way as a horse. äks′ ən

oys·ter *n.* An edible marine mollusk. ois′ tər

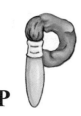

P

pass·port *n.* An official permission issued to a person allowing travel out of the country and return. pas´ pôrt

pa·tience *n.* The quality, state, or fact of being patient; being able to wait. pā´ shəns

pa·tients *pl. n.* People under medical care. pā´ shəns

pat·tern *n.* Anything designed or shaped to serve as a guide in making something else. pat´ ərn

peo·ple *pl. n.* Human beings. pē´ pəl

per·for·mance *n.* The act of performing. pər fôrm´ əns

per·sist·ent *adj.* Not giving up; enduring. pər sis´ tənt

per·son·al *adj.* Belonging to a person or persons. pur´ sə nəl

per·son·nel *n.* The body of people working for a business or service. pur sə nel´

phe·nom·e·non *n.* Something that can be observed or perceived. fə näm´ ə nän

pho·to *n.* A picture or image recorded by a camera. fōt´ ō

phys·i·cal *adj.* Relating to the human body, not including emotions. fiz´ i kəl

pleas·ant *adj.* Giving or promoting the feeling of pleasure; very agreeable. plez´ ənt

pock·et *n.* A small pouch within a garment, having an open top and used for carrying items. päk´ ət

po·ems *pl. n.* Compositions in verse with language selected for its beauty and sound. pō´ əmz

po·et *n.* A person who writes poetry. pō ət

po·et·ic *adj.* Having or using beautiful language. pō et´ ik

po·et·ry *n.* The art of writing stories, poems, and thoughts into verse. pō´ ə trē

pop·u·la·tion *n.* The total number of people in a given area, country, or city. päp yū lā´ shən

port·a·ble *adj.* Capable of being moved easily. pôrt´ ə bəl

por·tion *n.* A section or part of a whole; a share. pôr´ shən

pos·i·tive *adj.* Containing, expressing, or characterized by affirmation; very confident; absolutely certain; not negative. päz´ ə tiv

pos·sess *v.* To have ownership over something. pə zes´

post·date *n.* To date something with a date that is later than the current date. pōst´ dāt

post·grad·u·ate *adj.* Relating to study after high school or college. pōst graj´ ü ət

post·hu·mous·ly *adv.* After death. päs´ tyū məs lē

post·pone *v.* To put off; to defer to a later time. pōst pōn´

post·script *n.* Words written after a formal closing. pōst´ skript

post·war *adj.* During a period after war. pōst´ wôr

pow·er·ful *adj.* Possessing energy or great force; having authority. pou´ ər fəl

pre·am·ble *n.* An introduction to something, as a law, which states the purpose and reasons for the matter which follows. prē´ am bəl

pre·ar·range *v.* To arrange before. prē ə rānj´

pre·cau·tion *n.* A measure of caution taken in advance to guard against harm. prē kô´ shən

pre·cede *v.* To be or go before in time, position, or rank. prē sēd´

pre·date *v.* To date something with a date that is earlier than the current date; to come before the present time. prē′ dāt

pre·de·ter·mine *v.* To decide beforehand. prē di tur′ min

pred·i·ca·ble *adj.* Capable of being predicated. prē dik′ tə bəl

pref·ace *n.* The introduction at the beginning of a book or speech. pref′ əs

pre·heat *v.* To heat before. prē hēt′

pre·his·tor·ic *adj.* Relating to the time before recorded history. prē his tôr′ ik

prel·ude *n.* The opening of a musical program, an introductory action. prā′ lüd

pres·ence *n.* The state of being present. prez′ əns

pres·ents *pl. n.* Gifts. prez′ ənts

pre·view *n.* An advance showing or viewing. prē′ vyū

prize *n.* An award or something given to the winner of a contest. prīz

pro·duce *v.* To manufacture; to make; to present or bring into view. prə düs′

pro·duced *v.* Manufactured; made; presented or brought into view. prə düst′

pro·duc·tion *n.* The process or act of producing. prə duk′ shən

pro·tec·tive *adj.* Being in the state of protection or guarded. prō tek′ tiv

pub·lic *adj.* Pertaining to or affecting the people or community. pub′ lik

puz·zle *v.* To bewilder; to confuse. *n.* A toy, board game, or word game that tests one's patience and skills. puz′ əl

Q

quad·ri·ceps *pl. n.* The major muscles of the front of the thighs. kwä′ dri seps

ques·tion *n.* An expression of inquiry which requires an answer. kwes′ chən

R

rea·son·able *adj.* Having reason or logic. rē′ zən ə bəl

re·ceive *v.* To take or get something. rē sēv′

re·cent *adj.* Happening at a time just before the present. rē′ sənt

re·cess *n.* A break in the normal routine; a break during school for games. rē′ ses

re·cycle *v.* To use something again. rē sī′ kəl

reefs *pl. n.* Chains of rocks, coral, or sand at or near the surface of the water. rēfs

re·la·tion·ship *n.* A connection by blood or family; friendship; the condition of being connected. rē lā′ shən ship

re·li·a·ble *adj.* Capable to be relied upon. rē lī′ ə bəl

re·luc·tant *adj.* Hesitant. rē luk′ tənt

re·ply *v.* To give an answer. rē plī′

re·sent *v.* To feel angry about. rē zent′

re·spon·si·ble *adj.* Trustworthy; in charge. rē spän′ sə bəl

rock·et *n.* A device propelled with the thrust from a gaseous combustion. räk′ ət

roy·al *adj.* Relating to a king or queen. roi′ əl

S

sail *n.* A strong fabric used to catch the wind and cause a ship to move *v.* To travel on a sailing vessel. sāl

sale *n.* An exchange of goods for a price; disposal of items at reduced prices. sāl

salm·on *n.* A large, pinkish fish. sam′ ən

san·dal *n.* A shoe fastened to the foot by straps attached to the sole. san′ dəl

sax·o·phone *n.* A brass wind instrument having finger keys and a reed mouthpiece. sak′ sə fōn

scene *n.* A view; the time and place where an event occurs; a part of a play. sēn

sce·nic *adj.* Pertaining to natural scenery. sēn′ ik

sched·ule *n.* A list or written chart which shows the times at which events will happen, including specified deadlines. ske′ joo əl

schol·ar·ships *pl. n.* A grant given to a student to enable them to go to school. skä′ lər ships

sci·ence *n.* The study and explanation of natural phenomena in an orderly way. sī′ əns

sea·son *n.* One of the four parts of the year: spring, summer, fall or autumn, and winter; a time marked by particular activities or celebrations. sē′ zən

sea·way *n.* An inland waterway that leads to the sea. sē′ wā

seen *v.* To see something in the past. sēn

sem·i·an·nu·al *adj.* Happening twice a year. sem ī an′ yū əl

sem·i·cir·cle *n.* A half circle. sem′ ē sur kəl

sem·i·fi·nal *adj.* The game just before the final game. sem′ ē fī nəl

sense *n.* Sensation; feeling; the physical ability that allows a person to be aware of things. sens

sen·si·ble *adj.* Having sense or logic. sen′ sə bəl

sep·a·rate *v.* To divide or keep apart. sep′ ər it

se·quence *n.* The order or progression from one thing to another. sē′ kwens

serve *v.* To take care of; to wait on; to prepare and supply. surv

she'd *contr.* Short form of *she had* and *she would.* shēd

sheep *n.* A thick-fleeced mammal, domesticated for meat and wool. shēp

shouldn't *contr.* Short form of should not. shood′ nt

show·er *n.* A short period of rain; a bath with water spraying down on the bather. shou′ ər

shut·ter *n.* Covering for a window. shut′ ər

since *adv.* At a time before the present. *prep.* During the time later than. sins

skill *n.* Ability gained through practice; expertise. skil

so·cial *adj.* Having to do with people living in groups. sō′ shə

sol·emn *adj.* Very serious; characterized by dignity; sacred. säl′ əm

sought *v.* Looked for. sôt

spawn *n.* The eggs of fish or other water animals, such as frogs. *v.* To lay eggs. spôn

staffs *pl. n.* People employed to assist in the day-to-day affairs of running a business, organization, or government. stafs

stir *v.* To mix a substance by moving round and round. stur

strict *adj.* Holding to or observing rules exactly; imposing absolute standards. strict

stu·di·o *n.* The place of work for an artist, photographer, or other creative person. stü' dē ō

stu·di·os *pl. n.* Places of work for artists, photographers, or other creative people. stü' dē ōz

stum·ble *v.* To trip and nearly fall over something; to come upon unexpectedly. stum' bəl

sub·tle *adj.* To have a small or slight difference or change. sut' l

suc·cess·ful *adj.* Having a good outcome. sək ses' fəl

suf·fi·cient *adj.* As much as is needed or desired. sə fish' ənt

sum·mer·time *n.* The summer. sum' ər tīm

sur·ren·der *v.* To give up or yield possession or power. sər en' dər

swim·ming *v.* Moving the arms and legs in water. swim' ing

sym·pho·ny *n.* A large orchestra with wind, percussion and string sections. sim' fə nē

T

team·work *n.* A group of people working together toward a common goal. tēm' work

tel·e·cast *n.* A television broadcast. tel' ə kast

tel·e·gram *n.* A message sent or received by telegraph. tel' ə gram

tel·e·graph *n.* A system for communicating; a transmission sent by wire or radio. tel' ə graf

tel·e·phone *n.* A system or device for transmitting conversations by wire. tel' ə fōn

tel·e·scope *n.* An instrument that contains a lens system that makes distant objects appear larger and nearer. tel' ə skōp

that's *contr.* Short form of *that is* and *that has.* thats

their *adj. or pron.* Belonging to two or more things or beings previously named. ther

there *adv.* In, at, or about that place. ther

there's *contr.* Short form of *there is* and *there has.* therz

they're *contr.* Short form of *they are.* ther

they've *contr.* Short form of *they have.* thāv

thou·sand *n.* The number after nine hundred ninety-nine and before one thousand one. thou' zənd

thou·sands *pl. n.* Two or more thousands. thou' zəndz

thun·der·storms *pl. n.* Weather with rain, lightning, and thunder. thun' dər stôrmz

tide *n.* The rise and fall of the surface level of the ocean. tīd

tied *v.* Kept down with rope or some other strap-like device. tīd

toast *v.* To heat and brown over a fire or in a toaster. *n.* Sliced bread browned in a toaster. tōst

tow·er *n.* A very tall building or structure; a skyscraper; a place of security or defense. tou' ər

trans·port *v.* To carry or move from one place to another. trans pôrt'

tri·an·gle *n.* A plane figure with three sides and having three angles. trī' an gəl

tri·ceps *pl. n.* Muscles on the back of the arms. trī' seps

tri·cy·cle *n.* A small vehicle having three wheels, propelled by pedals. trī' si kəl

troupe *n.* A group of performers, actors, or singers. trüp

trout *n.* A fresh water fish. trout

tun·nel *n.* An underground or underwater passageway. tun′ əl

U

un·der·stand *v.* To comprehend; to realize; to know the feelings and thoughts of. un dər stand′

u·ni·corn *n.* A mythical animal resembling a horse, with a horn in the center of its forehead. yūn′ ə kôrn

u·ni·form *n.* Identical clothing worn by the members of a group. yūn′ ə form

u·nite *v.* To join or come together for a common purpose. yū nīt′

u·ni·ty *n.* The fact or state of being one. yūn′ ə tē

u·ni·verse *n.* The world, stars, planets, and space. yūn′ ə vurs

un·sta·ble *adj.* Not steady or firmly fixed. un stā′ bəl

ur·ban *adj.* Pertaining to a city or having characteristics of a city. ur′ bən

ur·gent *adj.* Requiring immediate attention. ur′ jənt

V

vac·ci·na·tion *n.* Medicine that protects against disease. vak sə nā′ shən

val·u·a·ble *adj.* Of great value or importance. val′ yū ə bəl

vane *n.* A metal device that turns in the direction the wind is blowing. vān

veg·e·ta·ble *n.* A plant, such as green beans or lettuce, raised for the edible part. vej′ tə bəl

vein *n.* A vessel that transports blood back to the heart after passing through the body. vān

ve·loc·i·ty *n.* Rapid speed. və läs′ ə tē

vis·i·ble *adj.* Apparent; exposed to view. viz′ ə bəl

voice *n.* The sound created by the vocal cords. vois

vol·ca·noes *pl. n.* Mountains with a crater where lava comes out of. vôl kā′ nōz

W

war·drobe *n.* A collection of clothes. wôr′ drōb

wash·able *adj.* Able to be washed. wäsh′ ə bəl

we'd *contr.* Short form of *we had* and *we would.* wēd

wheat *n.* A grain ground into flour, used to make breads and similar foods. hwēt

wheeze *v.* To breathe with a hoarse whistling sound. *n.* A high whistling sound. hwēz

when *adv.* At what time; at which time. *pron.* What or which time. *conj.* While. hwen

whis·per·er *n.* One who speaks quietly. hwis′ pər ər

wild·life *n.* Animals and plants living in their natural environments. wīld′ līf

wolves *pl. n.* More than one wolf. woolvz

wo·men *pl. n.* More than one female. wim′ ən

wrote *v.* Formed words or other symbols with a writing utensil. rōt

Parts of Speech

adj. = *adjective*
adv. = *adverb*
art. = *article*
conj. = *conjunction*
n. = *noun*
prep. = *preposition*
pron. = *pronoun*
v. = *verb*

Y

you're *contr.* Short form of *you are.* yoor

Answer Key

Page 6

Say each of the following words out loud, stressing the short vowel sounds. Then, write each word.

Spelling Tip: Short **a** is spelled **a**, short **e** is spelled **e** and **ea**, short **i** is spelled **i**. The symbol for short **a** is /a/. The symbol for short **e** is /e/. The symbol for short **i** is /i/.

Spelling Words

animal	animal
except	except
distance	distance
canyon	canyon
meadow	meadow
install	install
fantastic	fantastic
mention	mention
skill	skill
fraction	fraction
method	method
strict	strict
grand	grand
pleasant	pleasant
swimming	swimming

6

Page 7

Words in Context

Complete the paragraph below with spelling words.

Rocky Mountain National Park

In the middle of the splendor of the Rocky Mountains is one of America's most beautiful national parks. Visitors are amazed by the wild nature that surrounds them year-round. Don't be surprised if you encounter an **animal** in the park. Elk, deer, moose, bighorn sheep, black bears, coyotes, cougars, eagles, and hawks are common.

In the summer, a grassy **meadow** or hillside will show off their alpine wildflowers. Climbers can tackle challenging peaks. The park is home to 60 peaks with the elevation starting at a **distance** of 8,000 feet and going all the way to 14,259 feet. Climbers with much **skill** can climb over the tree-line. They are awed by a **grand** view of a **canyon** below. Trail Ridge Road, at 12,183 feet, is the highest continuous paved road in the United States.

In the summer, campers and backpackers enjoy the **pleasant** surroundings of the wilderness. All year long, visitors can enjoy **fantastic** wildlife viewing. Rocky Mountain National Park is a park for all ages and abilities.

Challenge

Circle the other words in the paragraph that have short **a**, **e**, and **i** sounds.

Word Building

A **gerund** is a verb form that ends in **ing** and is used as a noun. For example, the verb *write* can become a gerund when it is changed to *writing*. One spelling word can be a gerund. Write the word and its definition.

Word: **swimming**   Definition: the act or sport of a person who swims

7

Page 8

Fun with Words

Complete the crossword puzzle with spelling words.

Across
1. The mathematical expression ⅜ is called a _____.
3. The reporter told the artist he would _____ his name in the newspaper review.
4. The warm breeze coming off the ocean was a _____ ending to the evening.
7. The members of the track and field team had a _____ training schedule.

Down
2. The service technician was called to _____ the new telephone.
3. A _____ is a way of doing something or a process.
5. Holly liked all fruit _____ for raspberries.
6. _____ was Mikka's favorite sport.

Crossword answers: fraction, mention, pleasant, strict, install, method, swimming

Words Across the Curriculum

Write the social studies words on the lines.

1. discoveries **discoveries**
2. evidence **evidence**
4. excavation **excavation**
5. historic **historic**

Complete the following paragraph with the social studies words.

A Career as an Archaeologist

Do you like digging in the earth and making **discoveries**? If so, then archaeology may be for you. Archaeologists study **historic** people and places. they go on an **excavation** to find **evidence** from the past.

8

Page 9

Words in Writing

Write a paragraph about what career you want to have when you grow up. Use at least four words from this lesson.

Answers will vary.

Misspelled Words

Each of the following sentences has a misspelled spelling word. Cross out the misspelled word and write the word correctly above it.

1. A ~~meado~~ **meadow** is a low, level grassland near a lake or stream.
2. Rocky Mountain National Park is the home to many ~~animals~~ **animals**.
3. A ~~fraction~~ **fraction** has both a numerator and a denominator.
4. The word ~~except~~ **except** can be a preposition, a verb, or a conjunction.
5. ~~Swimming~~ **Swimming** is one of the best forms of exercise.
6. A ~~canyon~~ **canyon** is a long, narrow valley with high cliffs on each side.
7. ~~Evidence~~ **Evidence** is something that gives reasons or proof.
8. Scientists have made many important ~~discoveries~~ **discoveries**.
9. A citation made to honor or praise is an honorable ~~mention~~ **mention**.
10. The ~~distance~~ **distance** of a marathon is 26.2 miles.

9

Answer Key

Say each of the following words out loud, stressing the short vowel sounds. Then, write the words on the lines provided.

Spelling Tip — The short **o** sound can be spelled **o**. The short **o** sound can also be spelled **au**, **aw**, **oa**, and **ough**. These spelling are called *digraphs*. They have slightly different sounds. The symbols for short o are /o/ and / / (for the digraphs). The short **u** sound is spelled with the letter **u**. The symbol for short **u** is /u/.

Spelling Words

comedy	comedy
clumsy	clumsy
audience	audience
hundred	hundred
awkward	awkward
husband	husband
broad	broad
reluctant	reluctant
sought	sought
stumble	stumble
modern	modern
public	public
auditorium	auditorium
understand	understand
awning	awning

10

Words in Context
Complete the following sentences with spelling words.

1. The box was both tall and __broad__.
2. After graduation, the students __sought__ jobs in their fields.
3. Please be careful and don t __stumble__ on the ice as you leave the auditorium.
4. The play goers waited under the __awning__ to avoid the rain.
5. An __awkward__ moment followed after the actress momentarily forgot her lines.
6. At first, the children were __reluctant__ to go into the water.
7. Instead of antiques, the couple was looking for __modern__ furniture.
8. The parents could __understand__ their children s initial reluctance.
9. When my brother got married, he became a __husband__.
10. Everyone in the school had to go to the __auditorium__, because there was a pep rally for our basketball team.
11. I ve always wanted to be in a play. My favorite kind of play is a __comedy__.
12. We had a math test today. I got ninety-five right out of one __hundred__.
13. After Sonia and I finished our magic show and the curtain closed, we were nervous. The clapping and cheering that came from the __audience__ made us smile.
14. In the play, *The Crazy Clown*, the title character tripped over everything. He was extremely __clumsy__.
15. There were three dress rehearsals for the new play. But on opening night, the theater s doors were opened to the __public__.

11

Fun with Words
Complete this set by choosing spelling words to fill-in the blanks on the stage and the blanks in the dialogue.

Words Across the Curriculum
Write the science words on the lines beside each word.

1. clusters __clusters__
2. phenomenon __phenomenon__
3. spawn __spawn__
4. thunderstorms __thunderstorms__
5. unstable __unstable__

Complete the following paragraph with science words from above.

Thunderstorms

__Thunderstorms__ are an extremely common weather __phenomenon__. Thunderstorms can be only a few miles in diameter or can form __clusters__ that cover hundreds of miles. They usually occur in warm, humid conditions, although dry thunderstorms are common in the western United States. Dry thunderstorms can __spawn__ wildfires. When the air in a thunderstorm becomes __unstable__, or likely to quickly change, the storms can cause sever damage. However, only 10% of thunderstorms in the U.S. become this strong.

12

Words in Writing
Write a paragraph about a natural phenomenon. Use at least six words from this lesson.

Answers will vary.

Using a Dictionary
Words in a dictionary are listed alphabetically. Write the spelling words alphabetically.

audience	clumsy	public
auditorium	comedy	reluctant
awkward	hundred	sought
awning	husband	stumble
broad	modern	understand

13

Answer Key

Write each of the following words on the lines provided. Then, circle the letter or letters that give each word the short **a**, short **e**, or short **i** sound.

1. animal — **animal**
2. except — **except**
3. meadow — **meadow**
4. distance — **distance**
5. fantastic — **fantastic**
6. method — **method**
7. pleasant — **pleasant**
8. swimming — **swimming**

Complete the following narrative with words from above.

Claude and Todd were excited. They had been taking **swimming** lessons for years. Their school had a big meet this coming Saturday. Their coach had

taught them a new exercise **method**, and they felt they were getting

stronger. They had also been practicing going a longer **distance** than they would be required for the meet. They rode their bikes to school together on Saturday morning.

They passed an **animal** in a green **meadow** along the way. It seemed as if the pretty horse was wishing them well. It looked like if it would be a

pleasant day. They just hoped they felt the same way after the meet.

Everyone in the gymnasium was excited. Claude and Todd warmed up. The whistle blew and they hit the water. It was cold but that helped spur them on. Claude

felt strong. Todd felt good, **except** for a cramp he developed in his side. They both did well. Their relay team came in first. Claude had one other first place finish and two second place finishes. Todd had two second place finishes and one

third. They both knew they had done their best. They had a **fantastic** day.

14

Write each of the following spelling words. Then, circle the letter or letters that make this word have the short **o** or short **u** sound spellings.

1. comedy — **comedy**
2. auditorium — **auditorium**
3. awkward — **awkward**
4. broad — **broad**
5. sought — **sought**
6. clumsy — **clumsy**
7. modern — **modern**
8. reluctant — **reluctant**
9. audience — **audience**
10. awning — **awning**

Words from the above list are misspelled in the sentences below. Correctly rewrite the words on the lines after each sentence.

1. From the sound of the applause, the awdience must have loved the movie. — **audience**

2. Some of the students wore vintage clothes to the party, and some wore moadern attire. — **modern**

3. The graduate students saught an apartment with three bedrooms and a large kitchen. — **sought**

4. The uniform was too big and felt aukward to wear. — **awkward**

5. The couple couldn't decide if they wanted to see a coamedy or a drama. — **comedy**

6. The awditorium was not going to be large enough for the reception. — **auditorium**

7. The football player had broghd shoulders. — **broad**

8. The awkward chef was going to start his own television show, The Clomsy Cook. — **Clumsy**

9. The students were reluctant to start the long test. — **reluctant**

10. The sign on the auning announced the opening of the new play. — **awning**

15

Say each of the following words out loud, stressing the long vowel sounds. Then, write the words on the lines provided.

Spelling Tip	Long **a** can be spelled **a, ai, ay, ea, eigh,** and **a-consonant-e.** The symbol for long **a** is /ā/. Long **e** can be spelled **ea, ee, ei, ie,** and **y.** The symbol for long **e** is /ē/. Long **i** can be spelled **i, igh, y,** and **i-consonant-e.** The symbol for long **i** is /ī/.

Spelling Words

behavior	**behavior**
maintain	**maintain**
display	**display**
clean	**clean**
freight	**freight**
escape	**escape**
season	**season**
chimpanzee	**chimpanzee**
receive	**receive**
achieve	**achieve**
velocity	**velocity**
migrate	**migrate**
bright	**bright**
reply	**reply**
prize	**prize**

16

Words in Context
Complete the following paragraph with spelling words.

Chimp Life

Challenge

Circle the other words in the paragraph with the long **a**, **e**, and **i** sounds.

When you look at pictures of an ape, a gorilla, or a chimpanzee, do they look like they're looking right back and thinking about something? Well, most likely they are. Scientists have proven that chimpanzees are very

intelligent and **bright**. They have their own communication system. Scientists learned that studying chimpanzees in their own habitat was much better than in laboratories. In the field, scientists could study their true

behavior and habits. Chimpanzees live in groups and communicate to work together. If one chimp finds a food supply, he may jump in the trees and hoot to let others know where

to go. Staying **clean** is important to chimps. Grooming each other

communicates friendship. Chimpanzees also **display** affection for one

another with hugs. Other chimps **reply** with hugs, kisses, or hand shakes.

Chimpanzees use their sounds, gestures, and facial expressions to **achieve** communication with other chimps and with people, too. Scientists have taught chimpanzees to use sign language and the computer.

It's unfortunate that some of these intelligent and sensitive animals are in jeopardy. The forests where chimpanzees live are being destroyed. With help from conservation groups and protection agencies, hopefully the chimpanzees will

escape danger and prosper in their environments.

17

Answer Key

Fun with Words

Find seven spelling words in the following poem. Then, write the words under their appropriate categories. One word is used twice.

With the approaching season
The fleas planned to migrate
To a more temperate climate
Their tans they must maintain.

With swift velocity they sent
Their freight by way of the skies
The southern relatives would receive
Their northern cousins as a prize.

Long **a**	Long **e**	Long **i**
maintain	season	migrate
freight	receive	prize
migrate		velocity

Words Across the Curriculum

Write the social studies words on the lines.

1. body — **body**
2. chain — **chain**
3. great — **great**
4. lakes — **lakes**
5. seaway — **seaway**

Circle the letters in the social studies words that make the long **a**, **e**, or **i** sounds.

The Great Lakes consist of a chain of five lakes in Canada and the United States. The five lakes are Lake Erie, Lake Huron, Lake Michigan, Lake Ontario, and Lake Superior. These five lakes form the largest body of freshwater in the world. The lakes cover 95,000 square miles. The lakes were formed when the glaciers melted at the end of the Pleistocene period. In 1959, the St. Lawrence Seaway opened, connecting the Great Lakes with the Mississippi River and the Gulf of Mexico. This made the lakes an international body of water. The Great Lakes not only provide transportation for industry but also areas of great beauty in their parks.

18

Words in Writing

Write a poem or short story about nature using at least five of the spelling words.

Answers will vary.

Misspelled Words

Some of the spelling words are misspelled in the following paragraph. Cross out any misspelled words and rewrite them correctly above the misspelled word.

Why Do Animals Migrate?

Migration means that animals move from one location to another. Animals usually ~~migrate~~ **migrate** due to the changing of a ~~season~~ **season**. Some animals need to ~~escap~~ **escape** colder climates. They are looking to ~~maintane~~ **maintain** food and water supplies that come with warmer temperatures. Some animals in dry regions ~~migreight~~ **migrate** to ~~escap~~ **escape** droughts.

Migration may not always be necessary for adult animals, but babies need ideal conditions to ~~acheve~~ **achieve** the best care. Therefore, reproduction is most often the primary reason for seasonal migrations.

19

Say each of the following words out loud, stressing the long vowel sounds. Then, write the words on the lines provided. Over emphasize the difference between the /u/ and the / /.

Spelling Tip	Long **o** can be spelled **o**, **oa**, **ow**, and **o-consonant-e**. The symbol for long **o** is /ō/. Long **u** has two sounds. The /u/ sound is spelled **u** and has a y sound at the beginning of the vowel. The / / sound is spelled **u**, **ue**, **ew**, **oo**, **ou**, **u-consonant-e**, and **ui-consonant-e**. The difference between /u/ and / / is slight.

Spelling Words

condominium	condominium
coast	coast
below	below
mole	mole
humid	humid
studio	studio
blue	blue
drew	drew
cartoon	cartoon
troupe	troupe
attitude	attitude
toast	toast
growth	growth
universe	universe
costume	costume

20

Words in Context

Homographs are words that are spelled the same but have different meanings. Use spelling words to complete the following sentences. The words you use will be used twice for different meanings of the same word. Then, after you complete each sentence, write your own sentence using the word in the same context.

1. When you're going downhill, you can **coast** on your bicycle.
   Answers will vary.
2. The **mole** builds its home underground.
   Answers will vary.
3. Timothy sat down and **drew** a picture of a mountain range.
   Answers will vary.
4. The team felt **blue** after losing the tournament.
   Answers will vary.
5. My cousins live by the ocean, right on the **coast**.
   Answers will vary.
6. You should have that **mole** on your shoulder checked by a doctor.
   Answers will vary.
7. When the knight saw the dragon, he **drew** his sword.
   Answers will vary.
8. Her favorite color is **blue**.
   Answers will vary.

21

Answer Key

Page 22

Fun with Words
The following picture contains six spelling words. Look at the picture and then complete the sentences below.

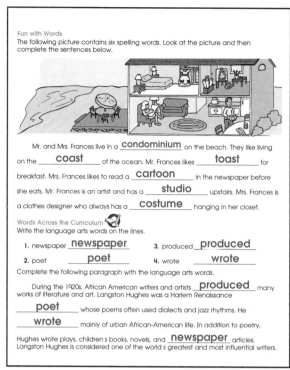

Mr. and Mrs. Frances live in a __condominium__ on the beach. They like living on the __coast__ of the ocean. Mr. Frances likes __toast__ for breakfast. Mrs. Frances likes to read a __cartoon__ in the newspaper before she eats. Mr. Frances is an artist and has a __studio__ upstairs. Mrs. Frances is a clothes designer who always has a __costume__ hanging in her closet.

Words Across the Curriculum
Write the language arts words on the lines.

1. newspaper __newspaper__   3. produced __produced__
2. poet __poet__   4. wrote __wrote__

Complete the following paragraph with the language arts words.

During the 1920s, African American writers and artists __produced__ many works of literature and art. Langston Hughes was a Harlem Renaissance __poet__ whose poems often used dialects and jazz rhythms. He __wrote__ mainly of urban African-American life. In addition to poetry, Hughes wrote plays, children's books, novels, and __newspaper__ articles. Langston Hughes is considered one of the world's greatest and most influential writers.

22

Page 23

Words in Writing
Create a cartoon strip. Draw figures inside each square and put dialogue in bubbles coming from the characters' mouths. Use at least four words from this lesson.

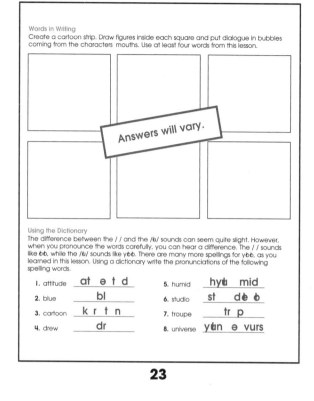

Answers will vary.

Using the Dictionary
The difference between the / / and the /ū/ sounds can seem quite slight. However, when you pronounce the words carefully, you can hear a difference. The / / sounds like ōō, while the /ū/ sounds like yōō. There are many more spellings for yōō, as you learned in this lesson. Using a dictionary write the pronunciations of the following spelling words.

1. attitude __at e t d__   5. humid __hyū mid__
2. blue __bl__   6. studio __st dē ō__
3. cartoon __k r t n__   7. troupe __tr p__
4. drew __dr__   8. universe __yūn ə vurs__

23

Page 24

4Write each of the following spelling words. Then, circle the letter or letters that make each word have the long a, long e, or long i sound.

1. behavior __behavior__   6. receive __receive__
2. freight __freight__   7. season __season__
3. maintain __maintain__   8. bright __bright__
4. achieve __achieve__   9. prize __prize__
5. chimpanzee __chimpanzee__   10. reply __reply__

Complete the following sentences with words from above.

1. The principal told the students to be on their __behavior__ during the pep rally.
2. Her dream was to __achieve or receive__ a medal in track and field.
3. The sun was __bright__, and the clouds were moving away.
4. The __freight__ was transported by ship.
5. The students were studying the behavior of the gorilla and the __chimpanzee__.
6. The best __prize__ at the fair was the stuffed teddy bear.
7. The students went to summer school to __maintain__ their spelling skills.
8. Charlie was hoping to __receive or achieve__ at least a B+ on his English paper.
9. Billy was waiting for a __reply__ from his college applications.
10. Autumn was quickly approaching, the __season__ of pumpkins and falling leaves.

24

Page 25

Write each of the following spelling words. Then, circle the letter or letters that make each word have the long o and long u sound.

1. condominium __condominium__   5. studio __studio__
2. coast __coast__   6. blue __blue__
3. below __below__   7. influential __influential__
4. universe __universe__   8. newspaper __newspaper__

Complete the advertisements below with words from above.

Classified Advertisements

FOR SALE

We have a beautiful two bedroom __condominium__ for sale. This condo is located in an __influential__ well landscaped neighborhood. The breakfast nook looks out onto the ocean __coast__. The living room has vaulted ceilings and a fireplace. The basement is perfect for an office or a workout room. You'll love the abundance of closet space. Contact the number listed in this __newspaper__ for more information on this find of the __universe__!

FOR RENT

We have an attractive __studio__ apartment for rent. This apartment is perfect for one person with an artistic flair. The skylights let in the sun and a view of __blue__ skies. A cozy kitchen is nestled beside the bedroom area. The fortunate renter receives free admission to the art gallery __below__ the apartment. Call the number listed in the __newspaper__ quickly, because this one will go fast!

25

Page 26

Say each of the spelling words out loud. Then, write each word.

Spelling Tip — Consonant digraphs are two or more consonant letters that together make one specific sound. Say each of the following consonant digraphs: **ch, ph, sh, th, wh.**

Spelling Words

champion	champion
alphabet	alphabet
accomplish	accomplish
athletic	athletic
wheat	wheat
check	check
photo	photo
finish	finish
marathon	marathon
when	when
chocolate	chocolate
physical	physical
shutter	shutter
thousand	thousand
wheeze	wheeze

26

Page 27

Words in Context
Complete the following article with spelling words. Not all of the words will be used, and some words will be used more than once.

What is a marathon?
A **marathon** is a long distance foot race.

How long is a marathon?
A marathon is 26.2 miles.

How did the marathon get its name?
The marathon received its name from the city of Marathon, Greece. According to legend, in 490 B.C. a runner named Pheidippides ran from Marathon to Athens, Greece (approximately 26 miles) carrying news of a battle victory over the Persians.

When was the first official race?
To celebrate the feat of Pheidippides, the first modern Olympics in 1896 held the first official marathon, retracing Pheidippides s route.

Who runs marathons?
Olympians train for marathons, as well as other professional athletes. But you don t have to be a **champion** to run marathons today. As running became more popular, recreational runners became interested in marathons as training for **physical** fitness, to achieve personal goals, and to test endurance. Today, tens of thousands of runners participate in marathons. What is thought of as a small race may have more than a **thousand** runners. It is still considered to be a **check** of athletic skill, with less than one percent of the world s population ever completing a marathon. Many people would **shutter** to think of running more than just a few miles, let alone more than 26 miles. It takes incredible **physical** and mental conditioning and training. But for those who have accomplished this task, all of the efforts more than pay off when crossing the **finish** line.

27

Page 28

Fun with Words
The bowl of soup contains all of the letters you will need to spell nine of the spelling words. Pick out and arrange the letters on the spoons below to spell out the nine words. You can use the letters more than once, but you cannot add letters.

Letters in bowl: B H T P Y K L W C R O K U A E S I Z

Spoon words: alphabet, athletic, wheat, check, photo, chocolate, physical, shutter, wheeze

Words Across the Curriculum
Write the social studies words on the lines. Use a dictionary if you need help defining any of the words.

1. empathy **empathy**   3. whisperer **whisperer**
2. friendship **friendship**

Complete the following paragraph with words from above.

A Horse Whisperer

Buck Brannaman is a horse **whisperer**. He has revolutionized the world of horse training and has paved the way for other trainers to follow. Brannaman s methods do not include breaking in a horse. His techniques involve forming trust and **friendship** with his horses. He shows **empathy**, a sharing of emotions and feelings. The horses respond and bonds are formed. Brannaman believes that listening to his horses is the best way to form a bond with them.

28

Page 29

Words in Writing
Write a paragraph about your friendship with a classmate, relative, or animal. Use at least five words from this lesson.

Answers will vary.

Misspelled Words
The following recipe contains misspelled spelling words. Cross out the words that are misspelled and rewrite them correctly above the misspelled words.

Chocolate
No Bake Champion ~~Chokolate~~ Oatmeal Cookies

2 cups	sugar	1 teaspoon	vanilla
3 tablespoons	cocoa	1 cup	coconut
⅓ cup	vegetable oil	3 cups	oatmeal
⅓ cup	2% milk		

If you decide to make this recipe, be sure you have adult supervision.

Mix sugar, coca, vegetable oil, and milk in a 2 quart glass bowl. Bring the mixture to a soft boil in the microwave for one minute. Add the remaining ingredients and stir. Drop by spoonfuls onto wax paper. **Finish** ~~Finis~~ by letting cool. Anyone can **accomplish** ~~accomplish~~ making these **champion** ~~champian~~ chocolate cookies. Sprinkle with powdered sugar and have your camera ready for the perfect dessert **photo** ~~foto~~.

29

Answer Key

Page 30

Say each of the words out loud. Then, write each word on the lines provided.

Spelling Tip Words with double consonants are often misspelled. Take extra time to remember how to spell those words.

Spelling Words

address	address
afford	afford
announcement	announcement
broccoli	broccoli
college	college
committee	committee
community	community
compassion	compassion
dilemma	dilemma
excellent	excellent
mirror	mirror
necessary	necessary
possess	possess
puzzle	puzzle
recess	recess

30

Page 31

Words in Context
Complete the following sentences using spelling words.

1. Make sure the __address__ is correct on the envelope before mailing it.
2. Let s jump rope at __recess__.
3. Can we __afford__ the new car?
4. I like to work the crossword __puzzle__ in the newspaper.
5. The students __possess__ many reading and math skills.
6. The __announcement__ of the new principal will be made at the next meeting.
7. Is it __necessary__ to fill out all of the forms?
8. __Broccoli__ is a very healthful vegetable.
9. Look in the __mirror__ before going out on stage.
10. My brother is going to play basketball in __college__ this year.
11. You received an A on your paper; that is an __excellent__ grade.
12. The homecoming __committee__ will vote on the decorations at their next meeting.
13. Having both play and baseball practice on the same night poses quite a __dilemma__.
14. Have you completed your __community__ service project yet?
15. The students have shown much __compassion__ to the animals we visited in the shelters.

31

Page 32

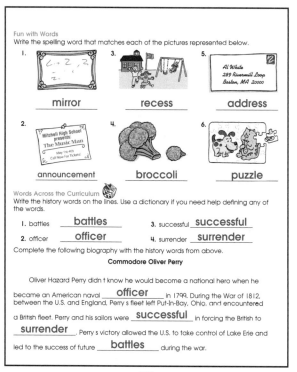

Fun with Words
Write the spelling word that matches each of the pictures represented below.

1. mirror
2. announcement
3. recess
4. broccoli
5. address
6. puzzle

Words Across the Curriculum
Write the history words on the lines. Use a dictionary if you need help defining any of the words.

1. battles __battles__
2. officer __officer__
3. successful __successful__
4. surrender __surrender__

Complete the following biography with the history words from above.

Commodore Oliver Perry

Oliver Hazard Perry didn t know he would become a national hero when he became an American naval __officer__ in 1799. During the War of 1812, between the U.S. and England, Perry s fleet left Put-In-Bay, Ohio, and encountered a British fleet. Perry and his sailors were __successful__ in forcing the British to __surrender__. Perry s victory allowed the U.S. to take control of Lake Erie and led to the success of future __battles__ during the war.

32

Page 33

Words in Writing
Write a dialogue with at least two characters. Write about a school event, an athletic event, a family event, or a community service project. Use at least six words from this lesson in your dialogue.

Answers will vary.

Using the Dictionary
Sometimes, a word will have more than one definition. Look up the following words in a dictionary. Write the definitions that match the use of the words in Words in Context on page 31.

1. address: _____
2. announcement: _____
3. afford: _____
4. committee: _____
5. community: _____
6. compassion; _____
7. dilemma: _____
8. necessary: _____
9. possess: _____
10. recess: _____

Answers will vary.

33

Page 34

Say each of the spelling words out loud. Then, write each word on the lines provided.

Spelling Tip
Sometimes, letter combinations produce silent letters. Say each of the following letter combinations with silent letters: **bt** (only the t is pronounced), **ck** (only the k is pronounced), **gu** (only the g is pronounced), **mn** (only the n is pronounced), and **sc** (only the s is pronounced).

Spelling Words

debt	debt
ascend	ascend
autumn	autumn
guardian	guardian
nickel	nickel
doubt	doubt
scenic	scenic
column	column
intrigue	intrigue
pocket	pocket
subtle	subtle
science	science
solemn	solemn
league	league
rocket	rocket

34

Page 35

Words in Context
Complete the following paragraph with spelling words.

A Career in Space

Imagine yourself soaring into the sky. As you __ascend__, you are above the clouds and into space. What a __scenic__ view! If thoughts of traveling in __rocket__ ships really interest you, then you should consider a career in the space industry. If you would like to follow in the footsteps of Neil Armstrong, John Glenn, and Mae Jemison, you can start by studying __science__, math, and even physical fitness in school. Space scientists must know a lot about biology, chemistry, physics, and mathematics. Those individuals who are fortunate enough to go into space must also be physically fit. __Subtle__ differences in physical ability can make a huge difference in successfully completing a training program.

If you love reading about space, but __doubt__ you're the type to walk on the Moon, plenty of careers are still open to you. Chemists, engineers, computer scientists, mathematicians, and even writers can all have careers full of __intrigue__ that deal with space. Writing a newspaper __column__ can make an astronaut famous. Most people who pursue a career in space, do so for the love of science and space. Joining the __league__ of space scientists in any capacity would be a rewarding life long career.

Word Building
Antonyms are words that mean the opposite of each other. Use a thesaurus or dictionary to find at least one antonym for each of the following spelling words.

1. ascend __descend__
2. autumn __spring__
3. doubt __trust__
4. solemn __light-hearted, informal__
5. subtle __obvious, strong__

Answers may vary depending on dictionaries used. Possible answers are given.

35

Page 36

Fun with Words
Unscramble the speling words on each leaf and rewrite them on the lines provided.

- taumun — autumn
- gaeule — league
- cinecs — scenic
- hertl / knleic — debt / nickel
- ctopek — pocket
- lemons — solemn
- dgluarna — guardian
- pocket
- solemn

Words Across the Curriculum
Write the social studies words on the lines beside each word.

1. guidance __guidance__
2. schedule __schedule__
3. scholarships __scholarships__

Complete the following sentences with words from above.

1. The __guidance__ counselors have many responsibilities.
2. They are responsible for helping students attain __scholarships__.
3. They also help students with their daily __schedule__.

36

Page 37

Words in Writing
Write a paragraph about a community service project you have either worked on or would like to work on. Use at least five spelling words.

Answers will vary.

Misspelled Words
The following sentences contain misspelled spelling words. Cross out the misspelled words and write them correctly at the end of each sentence.

1. After he received a raise, the borrower was happy to pay off his ~~depts~~. __debt__
2. Danny became a happy ~~gardian~~ of a shepherd mix puppy for the humane society. __guardian__
3. While out on a walk, Kari found one quarter, two dimes, and a ~~nikel~~. __nickel__
4. Rory and Betsy decided to take the ~~senic~~ route along the river on their way home. __scenic__
5. The table consisted of a dozen rows and a single ~~colum~~. __column__
6. The movie was full of suspense and ~~intrige~~. __intrigue__
7. Marissa liked the ~~poket~~ on the jeans. __pocket__
8. Brian was determined to join the baseball ~~leage~~. __league__

37

Page 38

Write each of the following spelling words. Then, circle the consonant digraphs.

1. champion — champion
2. chocolate — chocolate
3. photo — photo
4. physical — physical
5. accomplish — accomplish
6. finish — finish
7. athletic — athletic
8. marathon — marathon
9. wheat — wheat
10. when — when

Complete the following paragraph with words from above.

Louis Tucker was very __athletic__. His dream was to be a __champion__ in the state track and field event. He was willing to do whatever it took to succeed. His __physical__ fitness was very important. He trained every day. He watched his diet. His favorite food was whole __wheat__ pasta. __When__ the event was over, if all went well, he would reward himself with his favorite treat, __chocolate__ ice cream. Louis was very goal oriented. After finishing school, he dreamed of completing his first __marathon__. He could just picture the __photo__ of himself crossing the __finish__ line now. Louis had dreams to __accomplish__ quite a lot.

38

Page 39

Write each of the following spelling words. Then, circle the double consonants.

1. broccoli — broccoli
2. college — college
3. committee — committee
4. community — community
5. compassion — compassion
6. mirror — mirror
7. puzzle — puzzle
8. recess — recess

Write the word that matches each description using words from the list above.

1. a break from study or a hollow place in a wall — recess
2. a question or a problem or a game of skill and cleverness — puzzle
3. a vegetable. — broccoli
4. a place of higher studies or specialized training — college
5. a surface that reflects light — mirror
6. the need to help others — compassion
7. a group of people that studies and/or plans events — committee
8. a place where all of the people of a certain area live or a group of people who share common interests — community

Write each of the following spelling words. Then, circle the letter combination that forms the silent combination.

1. autumn — autumn
2. guardian — guardian
3. rocket — rocket
4. scenic — scenic
5. solemn — solemn
6. subtle — subtle

39

Page 40

Say each spelling word out loud. Then, write each word on the lines provided.

Spelling Tip	Vowel diphthongs are combinations of vowels that make a specific sound. This sound can be identified when comparing the following spelling words to each other. Some common vowel diphthong combinations are: oi and oy and ou and ow. The oi and oy diphthongs share a common sound and ou and ow share a common sound.

Spelling Words

appointment	appointment
coil	coil
coin	coin
joint	joint
choice	choice
employ	employ
enjoy	enjoy
oyster	oyster
royal	royal
cloud	cloud
house	house
mountain	mountain
crowd	crowd
shower	shower
tower	tower

40

Page 41

Words in Context

Complete the following paragraph with words from the spelling word list.

A Career in Physical Therapy

Have you ever thought about a job in physical therapy? People are staying active longer. What does this mean to our joints? Each __joint__ may wear down and an __appointment__ with a physical therapist may be in order. Physical therapists, by working with joints and muscles, help patients to move better and feel better. The __employment__ outlook for the field of physical therapy is quite good. Physical therapists work at hospitals, clinics, universities, corporations. They also have practices of their own. They work directly with injured people and their families. Not only is education important but physical therapists must also be kind and compassionate.

If you __enjoy__ working with people and are good at science, physical therapy may be a good career __choice__ for you.

Word Building

Suffixes are groups of letters that are added to the ends of words to change their meanings. The suffix -**ment** means action, process, or condition. Write the spelling word that has the -**ment** suffix and define it. Then, add the suffix -**ment** to two other spelling words and define the new words.

Word: __appointment__ Definition: the act of choosing someone for a position, an arrangement to meet someone or be somewhere at a certain time

Word: __employment__ Definition: the condition of being employed, one s work or profession

Word: __enjoyment__ Definition: the condition of having joy

41

Page 42

Fun with Words
Find the words from the box in the word search below. Words can be horizontal, vertical, diagonal, forward, and backward.

coil	house
coin	mountain
oyster	crowd
royal	shower
cloud	tower

```
m d w o r c m c
o y s t e r o o
u u n c h i k l
n i h n l s c n
t d u o l c o o
a t r l u r z b
i w e b a s b y
n b u n g y e e
r e w o t e o z
s h o w e r z r
```

Words Across the Curriculum
Write the social studies words on the lines beside each word.

1. boycott __boycott__
2. powerful __powerful__
3. voice __voice__

Complete the following paragraph with words from above.

What Is a Boycott?

A __boycott__ is the act of refusing to buy, sell, or use something. A historical example of a boycott is when the American colonists in 1765 avoided buying British goods after the passage of the Stamp Act.

The boycott of the Stamp Act worked. It was revoked in 1766. Today, people may boycott certain products if they don t agree on they way they are produced. For example, some people may boycott buying clothes if the manufacturers do not treat their employees well. Boycotts give a __voice__ to the public in a nonviolent, yet potentially __powerful__ way.

Page 43

Words in Writing
Write a paragraph about a school issue or an issue within your community. Use at least six words from this lesson.

Answers will vary.

Using the Dictionary
When looking up a word in a dictionary, you use **guide words** to help find the word you are looking for on the page. The guide words are the first and last word on a dictionary page. They are usually found on the top of each dictionary page. If the word you are looking for is between the two guide words, then it will be on that page. Look up the following words in a dictionary. Write the spelling word and then write the guide words on the lines provided.

1. appointment
2. coil
3. employ
4. house
5. joint
6. mountain
7. oyster
8. royal
9. shower
10. tower

Answers will vary.

Page 44

Say each of the spelling words out loud. Then, write each word.

Spelling Tip
The vowels **a**, **e**, **i**, **o**, and **u** can all be influenced by the letter r following them. Words with a **vowel+r** spelling make their own single-syllable sounds, with the r sound emphasized more than the vowel.

Spelling Words

department	department
determine	determine
stir	stir
director	director
bureau	bureau
larger	larger
pattern	pattern
first	first
historical	historical
disturb	disturb
wardrobe	wardrobe
serve	serve
inspiration	inspiration
humorous	humorous
urban	urban

Page 45

Words in Context
Each of the spelling words are scrambled below. Unscramble them, and then write them on the line.

Five isHtrolica __Historical__ Figures:
a reformer, an inventor, a politician, a poet, and a scientist

Henry Bergh — reformer (1811—1888)

Henry Bergh grew up in a rich and influential family. But something became more important to him than money. He felt awful when he saw animals overworked, neglected, or abused.

He wanted to terdemine __determine__ a solution and make a difference. It wasn t an easy task; he had to sidburt __disturb__ authorities and rsti __stir__ up favors from friends. In 1866, he opened the irfts __first__ organization in the United States to protect animals and enforce animal protection laws. This organization became known as the *American Society for the Prevention of Cruelty to Animals* (ASPCA). In 1874, Bergh created the Society for the Prevention of Cruelty to Children. Helping those in need was a tternpa __pattern__ all throughout his life.

George Washington Carver — inventor and scientist (1864—1943)

George Washington Carver began life as a slave and went on to become one of the most influential men of the 20th century. Carver received his college degree after earning his freedom from slavery. He became the rectordi __director__ of the rtDemepant __Department__ of Agricultural Research at Tuskegee University, a job he held his entire life. Carver devoted himself to bettering the economic conditions of the southern United States, specifically the welfare of African Americans. He is best known for his work with peanuts. He invented hundreds of uses for the peanut, as well as sweet potatoes, soybeans, and cotton.

Answer Key

Shirley Chisholm — politician (1924—2005)

Shirley Chisholm was the first African-American woman to be elected to the United States Congress. She served from 1969 to 1982. Before becoming a congresswoman, she was a consultant

to the New York City eauruB **Bureau** of Child Welfare. Chisholm was recognized nationally as an advocate for the nabur

urban poor. She was also the first woman to make

a serious attempt to vsere **serve** as president of the United States in the 1972 election.

Paul Laurence Dunbar — poet and novelist (1872—1906)

Paul Laurence Dunbar was the first African-American poet to receive international acclaim. Dunbar wrote hsuuomor

humorous poems about African-American life in the southern United States as well as many short stories, song lyrics, and novels. Dunbar s mother served as an nionistpair

inspiration to him. Although the Dunbar family did not have material wealth, they were rich in family support and a love of literature.

Albert Einstein — scientist (1879—1955)

Albert Einstein, born in Germany in 1879, was the first scientist to gain international popularity and fame. He won the Nobel Peace Prize for Physics in 1921. He was a pacifist, and he loved sailing and the violin. He was known to keep a small brodearw

wardrobe so as not to spend much time deciding what to wear. After his death, Einstein s brain was preserved and studied. It was discovered that part of his brain was missing, and

that another section had grown arlegr **larger**. The section that grew larger is responsible for mathematical thought.

46

Words in Writing

Write a biography about a historical figure who you admire. Use at least five of the words from the spelling word list.

Answers will vary.

Misspelled Words

Find the misspelled spelling words in the following sentences. Rewrite the words correctly on the lines provided.

1. Elise lived in a rural environment and Rebecca lived in an urbon setting. — **urban**
2. Don t forget to stur the soup every few minutes. — **stir**
3. The movie had a very humerous ending. — **humorous**
4. A bereau can be an agency that provides information or service, or it can be a chest of drawers. — **bureau**
5. Lionel s fourth grade teacher was a real insperation to him. — **inspiration**
6. The movie was made to disterb its audiences. — **disturb**
7. The students wanted to surve their community by participating in fundraising projects. — **serve**
8. Judith wanted to shop for a new spring wordrobe. — **wardrobe**

47

Say each word out loud. Then, write each word on the lines provided.

Spelling Tip	The /ə/ sound is an unaccented vowel. It can be found in any part of a word.

Spelling Words

exceptional	**exceptional**
camel	**camel**
castle	**castle**
identical	**identical**
easel	**easel**
dazzle	**dazzle**
mineral	**mineral**
label	**label**
example	**example**
original	**original**
level	**level**
people	**people**
sandal	**sandal**
tunnel	**tunnel**
visible	**visible**

48

Words in Context

Complete the paragraph below with spelling words. The first letter of each word has been provided for you.

Neuschwanstein Castle

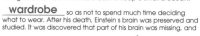

Do you think that Cinderella s Castle at Disney World in Florida is an

o**riginal** ? Cinderella s Castle was

patterned after a real c**astle** in Germany the Neuschwanstein Castle. King Ludwig of Germany began construction on his castle in 1869. The

e**xceptional** castle is

v**isible** as it peeks through the towering Alps that surround it. It is an

e**xample** of the Romanesque style with its turrets, balconies, and one

l**evel** above another. The interior is not i**dentical** to the

castle in Florida, but it will d**azzle** the eye. The castle is filled with

priceless murals, woodcarvings, and ornaments. Thousands of p**eople** visit the castle every year.

Word Building

Synonyms are words that have the same or similar meaning. Choose spelling words that are synonyms for the following words. Use a thesaurus or dictionary if you need help.

1. outstanding = **exceptional**
2. enchant = **dazzle**
3. exact = **identical**
4. model = **example**
5. flat = **level**
6. genuine = **original**
7. passage = **tunnel**
8. noticeable = **visible**

49

Spectrum Spelling
Grade 6

Page 50

Fun with Words
An easel is a stand that holds an artist's canvas. The pictures on each canvas represent a spelling word. Write the correct spelling word underneath each easel.

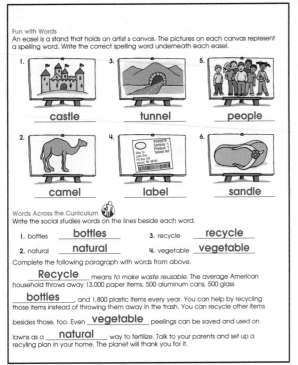

1. castle
2. camel
3. tunnel
4. label
5. people
6. sandle

Words Across the Curriculum
Write the social studies words on the lines beside each word.

1. bottles — bottles
2. natural — natural
3. recycle — recycle
4. vegetable — vegetable

Complete the following paragraph with words from above.

__Recycle__ means to make waste reusable. The average American household throws away 13,000 paper items, 500 aluminum cans, 500 glass __bottles__, and 1,800 plastic items every year. You can help by recycling those items instead of throwing them away in the trash. You can recycle other items besides those, too. Even __vegetable__ peelings can be saved and used on lawns as a __natural__ way to fertilize. Talk to your parents and set up a recyling plan in your home. The planet will thank you for it.

50

Page 51

Words in Writing
Write ten sentences below, using a different word from this lesson in each.

1. ___
2. ___
3. ___
4. ___
5. ___
6. ___ *Answers will vary.*
7. ___
8. ___
9. ___
10. ___

Using the Dictionary
Some vowels in unaccented syllables are represented by /ə/, called *schwa*. Look up the pronunciations of the following spelling words in a dictionary and write the phonetic respellings on the lines provided. Notice where the /ə/ is in each word.

1. camel — kam əl
2. castle — kas əl
3. easel — ē zəl
4. label — lā bəl
5. mineral — min ər əl
6. natural — nach ər əl
7. original — ə rij ə nəl
8. recycle — rē sī kəl
9. sandal — san dəl
10. tunnel — tun əl
11. vegetable — vej tə bəl
12. visible — viz ə bəl

51

Page 52

Say each of the words out loud. Then, write them on the lines provided.

> **Spelling Tip**
> Sometimes, the letters **ci** and **ti** make the /sh/ sound.

Spelling Words

ancient	ancient
immunization	immunization
commercial	commercial
infection	infection
efficient	efficient
innovation	innovation
especially	especially
introduction	introduction
glacier	glacier
portion	portion
social	social
production	production
sufficient	sufficient
question	question
vaccination	vaccination

52

Page 53

Words in Context
Complete the following paragraph with spelling words.

Vaccination

What is a __vaccination__?

Do you know the answer to that __question__?

Vaccination is a means of producing immunity against certain diseases through the __introduction__ of living or dead antibodies. In this way, the body's __production__ of less dangerous antibodies fights an __infection__. Vaccinations were used in __ancient__ times in China, India, and Persia. Edward Jenner proved that injecting just a small __portion__ of a virus into the skin was __sufficient__ to defend the body against viruses. This __inovation__ wiped out small pox and can prevent many other diseases. __Immunization__, which means to protect against disease __especially__ through vaccination, of 12 different diseases is recommended for children. Researchers are working to make a more __efficient__, one-dose vaccine for many diseases.

Word Building
Antonyms are words that have the opposite or close to the opposite meanings of each other. Write the spelling words that are antonyms for the following words. Use a thesaurus or dictionary if you need help.

1. modern = __ancient__
2. time-consuming = __efficient__
3. whole = __portion__
4. not enough = __sufficient__

53

Answer Key

Fun with Words
Find and circle the spelling words in the word search puzzle. They can be horizontal, vertical, forward, backward, and diagonal.

Words Across the Curriculum
Write the social studies words on the lines beside each word.

1. distribution   distribution
2. information   information
3. nation   nation
4. occupation   occupation
5. official   official
6. population   population

Complete the following paragraph with words from above.

The Census

Do you know the __population__ of your city or state? These figures are calculated with a census. A census is an __official__ count of the number of people in a city, state, or __nation__. Other __information__ gathered includes the age, gender, ethnicity, and __occupation__ of people in a specific area. The information gathered is used for a variety of purposes, including the __distribution__ of federal money. A census is taken every ten years in the United States.

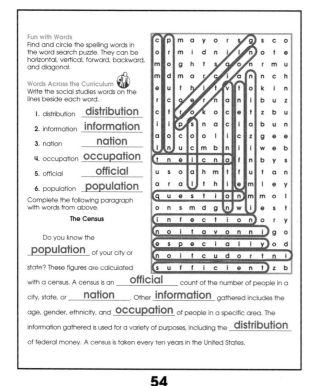

54

Words in Writing
Write a commercial of your own. Advertise one of your favorite products, such as your favorite tennis shoes, book, or movie. Use at least four words from this lesson.

Answers will vary.

Misspelled Words
The following commercial contains misspelled spelling words. Cross out the misspelled words and write them correctly above the misspelled words.

Commercial
Cruise Comercil

(close-up of a woman wearing a heavy jacket, as she speaks the camera pulls back and shows her standing near a big **glacier**)

Woman: Trying to decide on your next vacation? The sun and the beach just isn t the thing for you? The perfect vacation destination is waiting **especially** for you.

(the woman is walking on the decks of a ship glaciers behind her)

The grandeur of Alaska, with its **ancient** glaciers, amazing **population** of wildlife, and beautiful mountain peaks are right at your fingertips aboard the Midnight Sun Cruise Ship.

(shots of grizzly bears, moose, and gray wolves; shots of mountain peaks)

(interior shots of the cruise ship: dining room, pool, lounge chairs on deck)

When you re not in port enjoying the unique Alaskan towns and villages, you will be dining and relaxing aboard our **efficient** ocean liner. That is if you can pull yourself away from the decks. The sightseeing never ends, especially here in the land of the midnight sun.

(shot of Midnight Sun Cruise Ship s **official** logo)

55

Write each of the following spelling words on the lines provided. Then, circle the vowel diphthongs and the r-controlled vowel combinations.

1. coin   coin
2. royal   royal
3. house   house
4. mountain   mountain
5. tower   tower
6. wardrobe   wardrobe
7. service   service
8. first   first
9. humorous   humorous
10. disturb   disturb

Complete the following narrative with words from the list above.

High up on a __mountain__ lived Princess Katrina. She was the only daughter of a __royal__ family. She had everything a young princess could ask for: a beautiful __wardrobe__, many books, and extravagant jewels. But she was lonely. She spent most of her time alone in her room high in a castle __tower__.
One day, she heard laughter outside. The five students below were reading a __humorous__ play and laughing together. Princess Katrina wished she could live in a normal __house__ and go to a normal school. She quickly ran out of the castle and met the students on the path.
Princess Katrina pretended to be a new student in town. They told her about the community play they were all in. It was a play about a silver __coin__ found outside of a castle. Something seemed to __disturb__ the students, though. She found out that they were missing one person for their play. "I am at your __service__," said Princess Katrina. She then decided to tell them who she really was.
At __first__, the students were angry, but they realized that she was lonely and just wanted to have friends. Now, she had five friends!

56

Write each of the following spelling words on the lines provided. Then, circle the /e/ sound and the letter combinations that make the /sh/ sound.

1. mineral   mineral
2. camel   camel
3. example   example
4. original   original
5. tunnel   tunnel
6. castle   castle
7. ancient   ancient
8. immunization   immunization
9. glacier   glacier
10. question   question

Complete the following sentences with words from above.

1. A __question__ mark is a punctuation mark used at the end of a sentence.
2. A __mineral__ is a substance formed in the ground by nature, such as quartz, granite, and salt.
3. A large mass of ice and snow is called a __glacier__.
4. An animal that can store food and water for up to a few days is a __camel__.
5. A vaccination is a form of __immunization__.
6. The first of its kind is an __original__.
7. People who lived long ago are said have lived in __ancient__ times.
8. A large building that is home to kings and queens is a __castle__.
9. A train or car traveling in a passage underground is traveling in a __tunnel__.
10. An __example__ is a sample that explains a general rule.

57

Answer Key

Say each of the following words out loud. Then, write each word on the lines provided.

Spelling Tip	Compound words combine two complete words to make another word.

Spelling Words

backyard	backyard
birdbath	birdbath
butterfly	butterfly
classmate	classmate
classroom	classroom
everybody	everybody
everyone	everyone
everywhere	everywhere
hallway	hallway
homeroom	homeroom
hummingbird	hummingbird
outside	outside
summertime	summertime
teamwork	teamwork
wildlife	wildlife

58

Words in Context
Complete the following sentences using the spelling words.

1. We have many birds, squirrels, and chipmunks in our __backyard__.
2. Our class visited the __wildlife__ rehabilitation center on a field trip.
3. It took __teamwork__ to complete this huge project.
4. The __birdbath__ in the backyard gives the birds a place to drink and bathe.
5. It s fun to play outside in the __summertime__.
6. Did you see that __butterfly__ flutter by?
7. Let s play __outside__ while it is still light out.
8. My __classmate__ and I will complete the assignment together.
9. The __hummingbird__ moves so swiftly he is sometimes hard to see.
10. Can __everyone or everybody__ work on the same report at the same time?
11. I go to __homeroom__ first thing in the morning when I get to school.
12. __Everyone or Everybody__ must take their seat before class can begin.
13. The __hallway__ is quiet when class is in session.
14. The __classroom__ is full of busy students.
15. __Everywhere__ we look, we see examples of beautiful nature.

59

Fun with Words
Label the picture below using spelling words. Then, complete the paragraph describing the picture with other spelling words.

b u t t e r f l y

h u m m i n g b i r d   t e a m w o r k

b i r d b a t h

The __summertime__ is the best time to work __outside__. There is plenty of __wildlife__ to see in the __backyard__. After we go back to our __classroom or homeroom__, my __classmates__ and I will tell our teacher about the animals we saw.

60

Words in Writing
Write a paragraph about how you would create and maintain a backyard wildlife habitat. Use at least five words from this lesson.

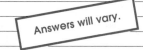

Answers will vary.

Using the Dictionary
Look up each individual word and write the definitions to these words and the compound words they make. The first one has been done for you.

1. bird = a warm-blooded animal with wings , two feet, and covered in feathers

    bath = the act of washing or dipping in water

    birdbath = a bowl with water set outside for birds to bathe in
2. home = __the place where one lives__

    room = __a space inside a building set apart with walls__

    homeroom = __the room where a class in school meets daily__
3. summer = __the season following spring__

    time = __the period between two events__

    summertime = __the time of year that is summer__
4. team = __a group of people working together__

    work = __doing or making something; labor__

    teamwork = __the action of people working together as a group__

Answers may vary depending on the dictionary used.

61

Answer Key

Say each of the following contractions out loud. Then, write each word on the lines provided.

Spelling Tip	Contractions are words that apostrophes ( ) substitute letters. Most contractions are made from forms of the verb *to be* (such as *is* and *are*); *had* and *have*; *could, should,* and *would*; *not*; and the phrase *let us.*

Spelling Words

it s	it s
that s	that s
there s	there s
you re	you re
they ve	they ve
could ve	could ve
he d	he d
she d	she d
we d	we d
doesn t	doesn t
don t	don t
hasn t	hasn t
mustn t	mustn t
shouldn t	shouldn t
let s	let s

62

Words in Context
The following dialogue contains words that could be written as contractions. Change the words to contractions from the spelling word list. Write them above the existing words.

> **Challenge**
> Circle the other contractions in this dialogue.

The Big Decision

you're
"Hey Lewis, you are in a big hurry. Where are you going?" yelled Lynda.

There's
(I'm) on my way to the post office. Can you come with me? There is one right
shouldn't
across the street and it should not take long," answered Lewis.
don't
"I do not see why not. On the way, maybe you can tell me what has you so excited."

could've
(I'm) sending in my application to be a junior counselor at camp, finally," replied
Lewis. "I could have sent it in sooner, but I waited because I was not sure what area I
it's
wanted to help. Mr. DeNune says it is time for us to think more seriously about our
We're
futures. We are in middle school, after all."
mustn't
"You must not keep me in suspense," laughed Lynda.

"Mr. DeNune told me to think about the kind of things I really enjoy."

I'm   That's
"Well, (that's) not hard to figure out," said Lynda. "You like baseball."
hasn't
"I am going to help the kids in little league. That is my idea of a good job. My dad
he'd
has not been happy that (I've) been putting off this decision. Now (he'll) be glad."
They've
"Well he would be proud of you right now," insisted Lynda.
Let's
"They've both got a reason to be proud,"
doesn't
said Lynda. "Let us hurry to the post office before it closes."

(We'll) make it," claimed Lewis. "It does not close for a
half an hour, (I'm) glad you came along, Lynda."

63

Fun with Words
Five of the contractions from the spelling word list have been scrambled in this pan. Use all of the letters and apostrophes to write the five contractions.

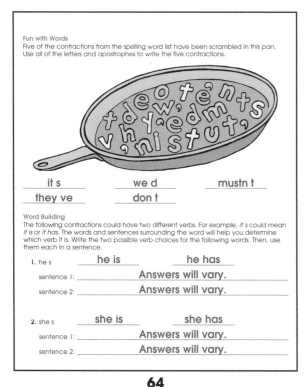

it s	we d	mustn t
they ve	don t	

Word Building
The following contractions could have two different verbs. For example, *it s* could mean *it is* or *it has*. The words and sentences surrounding the word will help you determine which verb it is. Write the two possible verb choices for the following words. Then, use them each in a sentence.

1. he s   he is   he has

sentence 1: Answers will vary.

sentence 2: Answers will vary.

2. she s   she is   she has

sentence 1: Answers will vary.

sentence 2: Answers will vary.

64

Words in Writing
Write a dialogue between at least two characters. The characters are trying to decide what they would like to do over summer vacation. Use at least six of the contractions from this lesson.

Answers will vary.

Misspelled Words
Some of the contractions in the following sentences are either misspelled or the apostrophe is in the wrong place. Cross-out the incorrect words and write them correctly on the lines provided.

1. ~~Lets~~ go to the library on our way home from school.   Let s

2. We ~~could~~ ordered pasta, but we decided on a pizza instead.   could ve

3. This book has very small writing and it ~~doesn t~~ have any pictures.   doesn t

4. ~~Shouldn t~~ we go to the earlier movie, since we have a game in the morning?   Shouldn t

5. Maybe we should change our plans. I here ~~there s~~ going to be a storm tomorrow evening.   there s

6. The teacher will check to make sure ~~youre~~ signed up for the field trip.   you re

65

Answer Key

Write each of the following spelling words on the lines provided.

1. backyard — **backyard**
2. classmate — **classmate**
3. classroom — **classroom**
4. everywhere — **everywhere**
5. hallway — **hallway**
6. homeroom — **homeroom**
7. outside — **outside**
8. summertime — **summertime**
9. teamwork — **teamwork**
10. wildlife — **wildlife**

Complete the following sentences with words from above.

1. Don t miss the bus or you may be late for **homeroom**.
2. Buddy went to the national park to see and learn about the **wildlife** that inhabits it.
3. Jason s **classmate** Sharon sits beside him in social studies class.
4. The school **hallway** is very crowded in between classes and at lunch.
5. Bert looked **everywhere** for his lost keys.
6. The students decorated their **classroom or hallway** for the spring festival.
7. Mora planted flowers and trees, and placed a bird feeder and birdbath in her **backyard**.
8. Alexie runs a lemonade stand in the **summertime**.
9. Since it stopped raining, the students went **outside** for recess.
10. Practice and **teamwork** are necessary to build a successful sports team.

66

Write each of the following spelling words on the lines provided.

1. it s — **it s**
2. that s — **that s**
3. you re — **you re**
4. they ve — **they ve**
5. he d — **he d**
6. she d — **she d**
7. doesn t — **doesn t**
8. don t — **don t**
9. hasn t — **hasn t**
10. mustn t — **mustn t**
11. shouldn t — **shouldn t**
12. let s — **let s**

Complete the following sentences with words from above.

1. The travelers **don t** know which way to turn, so they will have to stop for directions.
2. My mother said **she d** pick me up after play rehearsal.
3. **Let s** meet at the park Saturday morning.
4. **You re** going to bring water and snacks, aren t you, Mrs. Sopela? asked Sarah.
5. If we buy the movie tickets early, we **shouldn t or don t** have to wait in line.
6. The weather reporter said **it s** supposed to be nice all weekend.
7. We **mustn t or shouldn t** be late for our first day of classes.
8. Mr. Griss said **he d** take our class on a field trip next month.
9. My sister **hasn t** decided yet if she wants to play softball or run track.
10. Marty **doesn t** like chocolate ice cream; he prefers strawberry.
11. My aunt and uncle said **they ve** a cabin we can visit this summer.
12. I told my parents my plans for a summer job, and they said **that s or it s** a good idea.

67

Say each of the following plurals out loud. Then, write each word on the lines provided.

Spelling Tip

Most plurals are made by adding **s** to the singular form.
Words that end **consonant+y** change the **y** to **i** and add **es**.
Words that end in **vowel+o** add **s**.
Words that end in **consonant+o** add **es**.
Words the ending in **f** or **fe** and have the /f/ sound add **s**.
Words the end in **f** or **fe** and have the /v/ sound in it is plural change the **f** to **ve** and add **s**.

Spelling Words

letters	**letters**
thousands	**thousands**
databases	**databases**
languages	**languages**
cities	**cities**
dictionaries	**dictionaries**
libraries	**libraries**
flamingoes	**flamingoes**
studios	**studios**
dominoes	**dominoes**
volcanoes	**volcanoes**
reefs	**reefs**
staffs	**staffs**
bookshelves	**bookshelves**
calves	**calves**

68

Words in Context
Complete the following paragraph with spelling words.

Libraries

Did you know that there are **thousands** of libraries in **cities** all around the world. Public **libraries** have large reference sections with encyclopedias, periodicals, and **dictionaries**. You can even find historical essays, journals, and **letters** in libraries. They also have access to the Internet and large computer **databases**. Want to know about the world s active **volcanoes**? Do you know where to find coral **reefs**? Want to find out information on all kinds of animals, including **calves** and **flamingoes**? Do you want to learn how to play **dominoes**? You can find all these answers at a library.

Books in many **languages** can typically be found in college libraries. College libraries also sometimes have audio **studios** where visitors can listen to CDs and audiotapes.

Special libraries are run by corporations, governments, and organizations. Some libraries are solely devoted to one subject area. Regardless of the type of library you visit, they all have rows and rows of **bookshelves**.

The excellent **staffs** at every library are very helpful and are always willing to help you find the information you are looking for.

69

Answer Key

Fun with Words
See how many of the dominoes you can knock over by answering the riddle inside of each box with a spelling word

Our insides are alphabetized and defined.	Oceans and borders may change us, but anyone can learn more than one of us.	Many famous photographers, artists, and actors have passed through us.	We are sat on by very smart and interesting objects.	We re oblong on the outside and dotted on the inside.
dictionaries	languages	studios	bookshelves	dominoes

Words Across the Curriculum
Write the social studies words on the lines beside each word.

1. airplanes **airplanes**
2. beavers **beavers**
3. eagles **eagles**
4. ferries **ferries**
5. wolves **wolves**

Complete the following paragraph with words from above.

The Wolves of Isle Royale

Imagine trying to cross an enormous lake with no **airplanes** or **ferries**. That would be pretty hard. Fortunately for a female wolf during the winter of 1948—1949, the lake froze. The wolf crossed Lake Superior to Isle Royale, Michigan. Now, there are three packs of **wolves** there. These wolves prey on the moose of the island. In fact, the island is well known for its 45-year-long predator-prey study. The island, a designated wilderness area, is also home to bald **eagles**, ospreys, and **beavers**.

70

Words in Writing
Write five riddles whose answers are words from this lesson.

Answers will vary.

Using the Dictionary
Below are five words from this lesson and their singular forms that end in the letter **f**.
Look up the singular and plural forms in the dictionary and write their pronunciations.

1. bookshelf: **book shelf**
   bookshelves: **book shelvz**
2. calf: **kaf**
   calves: **kavz**
3. reef: **rēf**
   reefs: **rēfs**
4. staff: **staf**
   staffs: **stafs**
5. wolf: **woolf**
   wolves: **woolvz**

71

Say each of the following plurals out loud. Then, write each word on the lines provided.

Spelling Tip	Some words do not have a regular plural form. These words must be memorized.

Spelling Words

children	children
geese	geese
men	men
mice	mice
oxen	oxen
people	people
media	media
women	women
bass	bass
cod	cod
deer	deer
moose	moose
salmon	salmon
sheep	sheep
trout	trout

72

Words in Context
Cross out the singular words that should be plural and write the correct plural spelling word above them. Some words are used more than once.

~~Woman~~ **Women** dress in their fanciest clothes. ~~Man~~ **Men** even wear tuxedoes. The ~~child~~ **children**, both boys and girls, dazzle the crowds. They are ready for their walk down the red carpet. Who are they? They are the actors, writers, directors, producers, and craftspeople who are nominated for an Emmy award. Millions of ~~person~~ **people** from all over the world watch the Emmy award presentations on television. The Emmy awards are given to those professionals who have shown excellence in television. The Emmy s Hall of Fame includes over 100 ~~man~~ **men** and ~~woman~~ **women**. These ~~person~~ **people** have made a significant impact on how television, of all the ~~medium~~ **media**, has changed the lives of the mass audiences who view it.

73

Spectrum Spelling
Grade 6

Answer Key

Page 74

Fun with Words

The clues below tell you who is talking in this wilderness scene. The names of the animals are scrambled in the sentences. Unscramble the spelling words to answer the questions.

1. Whether one fish or more, we go by the name cdo **cod**, and we are large fish found in the northern seas.

2. If one of us has wondered off, we d be a goose, but when we re swimming together, we re called egese **geese**

3. We re large animals who live in northern regions and whether one or more, we re called somoe **moose**

4. We live in the ocean but swim up river to lay our eggs. One of us, as well as a group of us, is called a lamosn **salmon**

5. One or more, we re called pehes **sheep**, and we re related to goats.

6. One small rodent with small ears and a long, thin tail is called a mouse, but when we re with our friends, we re called cemi **mice**

7. We re a small fish in the salmon family who live in lakes, streams, and rivers. One or more, we re called rotut **trout**

8. We can run swiftly through the woods and whether we are alone or together, we re called rede **deer**

9. We can live in freshwater or saltwater, and whether one or more of us are swimming in the North American waters, we re called sabs **bass**

10. One of us is called an ox, but more than one of a group of farm animals is called xeno **oxen**

74

Page 75

Words in Writing

Write five sentences using a different spelling word in each.

1. _____
2. _____
3. _____ *Answers will vary.*
4. _____
5. _____

Words Across the Curriculum

Write the social studies words on the lines beside each word.

1. bread   **bread**   4. corn   **corn**
2. wheat   **wheat**   5. rye   **rye**
3. barley   **barley**

In the paragraph below, cross out the incorrect plural spellings and write them correctly above it.

Food can vary greatly from one region of the world to the next. However, one food that almost every culture has in common is bread. ~~Breads~~ **Bread** was critical to ancient civilizations because it could be made in the summer and stored all winter.

During the Stone Age, people crushed the grains of ~~barleys~~ **barley** and ~~wheats~~ **wheat** with stones. ~~Breads~~ **Bread** was such an important part of the lives of the Egyptians that they buried loaves in Egyptian tombs. When early American settlers lacked the ~~wheats~~ **wheat** and ~~ryes~~ **rye** grains of Europe, the Native Americans taught them how to make bread from ~~corns~~ **corn**

75

Page 76

Say each of the following possessives out loud. Then, write each word on the lines provided.

Spelling Tip	**Possessives** show possession, or ownership. To spell the possessive of a singular noun, add an apostrophe and an **s**. To spell the possessive of plural nouns ending in **s**, add an apostrophe after the **s**. If the plural noun does not end in an **s**, add both the apostrophe and an **s**.

Spelling Words

coach s	**coach s**
coaches	**coaches**
director s	**director s**
directors	**directors**
guide s	**guide s**
guides	**guides**
player s	**player s**
players	**players**
referee s	**referee s**
referees	**referees**
roommate s	**roommate s**
roommates	**roommates**
student s	**student s**
students	**students**
teeth s	**teeth s**

76

Page 77

Words in Context

Cross out the possessives with the incorrectly placed apostrophes and rewrite them correctly above the incorrect words. Underline the spelling words that are used correctly.

Dear Celina,

How are you? I'm writing to you from the end of my first week at summer camp. Both of my **roommates'** ~~roommate's~~ closets are bigger than mine. But they've been here before and had first pick. Sisters can share rooms. Next year, you'll be old enough to come, too. We have many activities to choose from. We're even going to put on a play. I didn't get off to a great start with the director though. At practice last night, I sat in the **director's** ~~directors~~ chair. He was nice about it, though.

My favorite activity so far has been softball. Our first game was yesterday. By the second inning, it was pouring rain. All of the **players'** ~~players~~ uniforms were covered in mud. One of the **referee's** ~~referees~~ shirts was so muddy you couldn't tell the white strips from the black ones. All of the <u>referees'</u> whistles blew water—it was funny. My team played really well and won by two runs. We poured a pitcher of water on our **coach's** ~~coachs~~ jacket after we won the game. But I don't think he minded—he was really muddy, too. Both <u>coaches'</u> families came to watch our game so we had support.

I've also enjoyed our nature hikes. I'm learning a lot about the environment. Someday, I would like to be a guide, too. Our nature **guide's** ~~guides~~ son came along with us. It's amazing how much he knows!

See you in a week!

Love, Janine

77

Answer Key

Page 78

Fun with Words
Choose spelling words that complete the following sentences and fit in the boxes. Write the words in the boxes. Don t forget the apostrophes.

1. The _____ grades got better after he was told he couldn t play basketball.

s	t	u	d	e	n	t		s

2. The _____ good condition can be attributed to daily care and proper dentist visits.

	t		e		e	t	h		s

3. Charlotte s _____ desk was always cluttered.

r	o	o	m	m	a	t	e		s

4. The _____ association made sure their members were honest and fair in all games.

r	e	f	e	r	e	e		s

or referees

Words Across the Curriculum
Write the science words on the lines beside each word.

1. animal s   **animal s**   3. male s   **male s**
2. moose s   **moose s**

Insert an apostrophe to correct the spelling words below.

What **animal s** body is large and brown and has front legs that are larger than its back legs? It is a moose. A moose is the largest member in the deer family. A **moose s** habitat is in northern parts of Eurasia and North America. An adult **male s** weight can reach 1,800 pounds. A moose is protected in the national parks and reserves of both the United States and Canada.

Page 79

Words in Writing
Write a letter to your best friend. Tell your friend about school, family, or community events. Use at least five words from this lesson.

Answers will vary.

Using the Dictionary
Adding the possessive **s** to a word gives the word the same sound as its plural form. Some words add an /s/ sound, as in *coach s*. Other words add a /z/ sound, as in *guide s*. Use a dictionary to look up and write the phonetic spellings of each word. Say the word out loud and add either an **s** or a **z** to the end of the phonetic spellings to add the possessive sound. The first one has been done for you.

1. coach s   kōch es
2. coaches   kōch es
3. director s   də rek tərz
4. directors   də rek tərz
5. guide s   gīdz
6. guides   gīdz
7. player s   plā ərz
8. players   plā ərz
9. referee s   ref ə rēz
10. referees   ref ə rēz
11. roommate s   r̄m māts
12. roommates   r̄m māts
13. student s   st̄d nts
14. students   st̄d nts
15. teeth s   tēths

Page 80

Write each of the following spelling words on the lines provided. For the regular plurals, circle the **s** or **es** that makes the word plural. Do not circle anything in the irregular plurals.

1. thousands   thousand(s)
2. libraries   libraries
3. studios   studio(s)
4. volcanoes   volcano(es)
5. reefs   reef(s)
6. bookshelves   bookshelves
7. children   children
8. geese   geese
9. mice   mice
10. people   people
11. salmon   salmon
12. sheep   sheep

The words from the above list are misspelled in the following paragraph. Cross out the misspelled words and rewrite them correctly above the misspelled word.

Thousands of **people** visit school **libraries** every year. They scour the **bookshelves** looking for information on everything from accordions to **volcanoes**. One student is going to be a veterinarian and open an animal sanctuary and wildlife rehabilitation center. She uses the library to study **geese** cows, pigs, **sheep**, **mice** and fish, like **salmon**. Another student is studying education. He wants to help **children** who have disabilities. He's going to be a coach for the Special Olympics. Another student wants to go into marine biology. He wants to help protect the whales and other sea life. Currently, he is studying the ocean **reefs**. Yet another student is studying different languages. She uses the audio and video **studios** to watch and listen to foreign language dialogues. She wants to teach languages in other countries. Libraries are available to everyone to study and learn. Then, those who learn can teach others who will also benefit from the library system.

Page 81

Write each of the following spelling words on the lines provided. Circle the apostrophe or the **'s** that make each word possessive.

1. coach's   coach('s)
2. coaches'   coaches(')
3. guide's   guide('s)
4. guides'   guides(')
5. player's   player('s)
6. players'   player(')
7. roommate's   roommate('s)
8. roommates'   roommates(')
9. student's   student('s)
10. students'   students(')

The words in the above list are scrambled in the following sentences. Unscramble them and write them on the lines provided. Do not forget the apostrophes.

1. Kay likes borrowing her only mormotase' **roommate's** clothes.
2. The four torm'eosam **roommates'** kitchen was nicely stocked with soda pop and snacks.
3. The museum d'iguse **guide's** microphone was not working.
4. All of the nature sedig'u **guides'** trail maps were always accurate and up to date.
5. The basketball hoc'acs **coach's** behavior was inappropriate at the game.
6. The yearbook displayed all of the c'ahocse **coaches'** photographs in one section.
7. The golf yepul'rs **player's** caddy had been with him for years.
8. Both tennis la'yreps **players'** outfits were corporately sponsored.
9. That sudetns't **student's** best friend was moving to another state.
10. All of the tedusnst' **students'** homework was due first thing in the morning.

Say each of the following words out loud. Then, write each word on the lines provided.

Spelling Tip	A **prefix** is a group of letters that is added to the beginning of a base word to change its meaning. The prefix **pre-** means *before*. The prefix **post-** means *after*.

Spelling Words

preamble	preamble
prearrange	prearrange
precaution	precaution
precede	precede
predate	predate
predetermine	predetermine
preface	preface
preheat	preheat
prelude	prelude
preview	preview
postdate	postdate
postgraduate	postgraduate
postpone	postpone
postscript	postscript
postwar	postwar

82

Words in Context
Complete each sentence with a spelling word.

1. If you see a movie ahead of time, you are seeing the __preview__ .
2. The part at the beginning of a document that states its reason is the __preamble__ .
3. To write a date that is after the current date is to __postdate__ an item.
4. The part that comes before a musical is the __prelude__ .
5. Arranging a meeting ahead of time means to __prearrange__ the meeting.
6. Adding a note after the signature is adding a __postscript__ .
7. The chef will __preheat__ the oven before she s ready to bake the pie.
8. Taking action ahead of time against danger is taking a __precaution__ .
9. A class one takes or studies after graduation is a __postgraduate__ class.
10. The remarks made at the beginning of a book is the __preface__ .
11. To go or come before in time or order is to __precede__ .
12. If an umpire was to __postpone__ the game, he would be delaying it.
13. To decide ahead of time is to __predetermine__ .
14. After a war is the __postwar__ period.
15. Writing a date that is before the current date is to __predate__ an item.

83

Fun with Words
Chef Brian must choose the right word from each bottle in order to correctly complete the story. Write the correct word on the lines provided.

1. predetermine | predate
2. postscript | preview
3. precaution | preamble
4. postdate | preheat
5. preface | prearrange
6. postpone | preheat

The chef needs to (1) __predetermine__ what he wants to serve for dinner. First, he needs to (2) __preview__ the recipe. He decides to take (3) __precaution__ and (4) __preheat__ the oven. Oh, no! He forgets to read the (5) __preface__ at the beginning of the recipe and pours his ingredients in a pan before flouring it. The chef must (6) __postpone__ the dinner until he has time to start again.

Words Across the Curriculum
Write the social studies words on the lines beside each word.

1. prehistoric __prehistoric__   2. posthumously __posthumously__

Complete the following sentences with words from above. Use a dictionary if you need help.

1. __Posthumously__ means after something has died.
2. __Prehistoric__ means the time before written history.

84

Words in Writing
Write eight sentences using a different word from this lesson in each.

Answers will vary.

Misspelled Words
Some of the words in the following news broadcast are misspelled. Cross out the misspelled words and rewrite the words correctly above the misspelled words.

Hi! This is Andrea Delmonic standing outside the City Theater. I m waiting for the audience who is here to __preview__ this summer s latest blockbuster to emerge. Here they come now. Excuse me, sir, what do you think of the action-packed musical documentary?

It was fantastic! I encourage all future theater goers to __prearrange__ your schedules and buy tickets early.

Miss, what did you think of this musical set in the postwar period?

Don t be late to this one. The __prelude__ is one of the best parts!

You heard it here first. Don t __postpone__ seeing this year s biggest movie. I know I won t! This is Andrea Delmonic, entertainment reporter for *Movie News*.

85

Answer Key

Say each of the following words out loud. Then, write each word on the lines provided.

Spelling Tip	The prefixes **im-** and **in-** both can mean *not*.

Spelling Words

imbalance	imbalance
inaccurate	inaccurate
immature	immature
inactive	inactive
immeasurable	immeasurable
incapable	incapable
imperfect	imperfect
inconsiderate	inconsiderate
impossible	impossible
indecisive	indecisive
impolite	impolite
indirect	indirect
improper	improper
inexpensive	inexpensive
informal	informal

86

Words in Context

Complete the following paragraph with spelling words. Not all of the words will be used. Words are not used more than once.

Pirates!

Pirates behavior was seen as **improper**. They were sometimes known to be **inconsiderate**. Some people of the time thought them **incapable** of being upstanding citizens. But many of the reports of these **impolite** thieves and marauders might have been **innacurate**, not necessarily telling the whole truth.

Many pirates were former navy men. Life in the navy was brutal, and it was **impossible** to leave the service once you began. Therefore, if a navy ship was captured by pirates, some navy men became pirates themselves.

Pirates, who sometimes preferred fancy clothes to **informal** ones, had the opportunity to become rich. Pirates were sometimes hired by governments to raid ships of opposing countries. These pirates were called *privateers*.

Pirates caused **immeasurable** harm to people and property. However, some positive, **indirect** benefits did come from piracy. At the time, there was an **imbalance** in trade throughout the western world, as most goods were going to a few places. Piracy led to more open trade routes as goods were taken from one colony to another.

The words improper, immature, and impolite can be interchanged.

87

Fun with Words

Unscramble the spelling words in the following sentences.

1. The banker concluded that the figures were ncuaeiacrt **innacurate**.

2. The volcano remained evitcani **inactive**.

3. The pomietil **impolite** man was nosdrteaeinci **inconsiderate** to others.

4. The T-shirts were relatively inpenexsive **inexpensive**.

5. The dress for the dance was going to be lamrofni **informal**.

Words Across the Curriculum

Write the science words on the lines beside each word.

1. immersed **immersed**   3. infected **infected**
2. immobilize **immobilize**   4. inhale **inhale**

Complete the following paragraph with words from above. Use a dictionary if you need help.

The medic on the scene had to act quickly when the cyclist in the race fell off his bike. It looked like his wrist may be broken. First, she made sure to **immobilize** the wrist with a sling. A finger on his other hand had begun to swell. The medic carefully **immersed** his finger in a bucket of ice. Then, she asked him to **inhale**. This next part was going to hurt a bit. The scratch on his knee may become **infected**, and she needed to put alcohol on it. This was going to sting. But the cyclist was tough.

88

Using the Dictionary

Put the words from this lesson in alphabetical order. Then, write a brief definition for each.

1. imbalance
2. immature
3. immeasurable
4. immersed
5. immobilize
6. imperfect
7. impolite
8. impossible
9. improper
10. inaccurate
11. inactive
12. incapable
13. inconsiderate
14. indecisive
15. indirect
16. inexpensive
17. infected
18. informal
19. inhale

Answers will vary.

89

Answer Key

Say aloud each of the following words. Then, write each word on the lines provided.

Spelling Tip	Some prefixes express a specific number or quantity. The prefixes **hemi-** and **semi-** mean *half*. The prefix **uni-** means *one*. The prefix **bi-** means *two*. The prefix **tri-** means *three*.

Spelling Words

hemisphere	hemisphere
hemicycle	hemicycle
semiannual	semiannual
semicircle	semicircle
semifinal	semifinal
unicorn	unicorn
uniform	uniform
universe	universe
biweekly	biweekly
bicycle	bicycle
bifocals	bifocals
binoculars	binoculars
biplane	biplane
triangle	triangle
tricycle	tricycle

90

Words in Context
Complete the following journal entry with spelling words. One word is used twice.

September 13

Science class was interesting today. We are studying the **universe** and all of its planets and stars. I like learning about the planets. The whole class seemed into it. Mr. Deibert had the class sit in a **semicircle**, or as Mrs. Richards would say, **hemicycle**. He set out different sizes of balls to represent the planets in relation to the Earth, sun, and Moon.

After we finish this unit, we re going to study the Earth and the Western **Hemisphere** and the Eastern **Hemisphere**. I can t believe that when it s summer in this hemisphere, it s winter in the other. I want to go there when it s winter here so I can have summer all year long! Then, I could ride my **bicycle** on the trails without any snow.

This Saturday is our first soccer game. I ll pick up my new **uniform** after school tomorrow. I like our colors: blue and yellow. I think our team is going to be great this year. I m sure we ll make it to the **semifinal** game again this year.

This Sunday, I m going on a hike with my dad. We re going to look for birds and log them in a book. He says he has a present for me. I think it is a pair of **binoculars**. I kept borrowing his on our last hike. I don t think he minded, but it will be nice if we both have a pair to look at the far away birds.

Well, that s it for today. I have more math homework to do tonight. We re studying shapes in geometry, like the **triangle** and the hexagon. It s hard but kind of interesting. Better go!

91

Fun with Words
Match the prefixes on the left with the pictures on the right to make spelling words.

1. bi — biweekly
2. tri — tricycle
3. hi — bifocals
4. semi — semiannual
5. bi — biplane
6. uni — unicorn
7. hemi — hemisphere
8. bi — binoculars

Words Across the Curriculum
Write the science words on the lines beside each word.

1. biceps — biceps
2. quadriceps — quadriceps
3. triceps — triceps

Complete the following sentences with words from above.

1. The muscles in the body with three heads at the back of the arm are called the **triceps**.
2. Muscles with two heads at the front of the arm are called the **biceps**.
3. Large muscles in the lower body with four heads in the front of the thighs are called the **quadriceps**.

92

Words in Writing
Write two or three sentences about one of your favorite exercises or sports. Use at least three words from this lesson.

Answers will vary.

Misspelled Words
Rewrite the misspelled spelling words correctly on the lines provided.

1. A hemicicle means the same thing as a semicircle. — hemicycle
2. If the doctor asks you to visit on a semiannual basis she wants to see you twice a year. — semiannual
3. Some schools require students to wear a unform; so all of the students wear the same clothes. — uniform
4. If employees receive paychecks byweekly, they receive their checks once every two weeks. — biweekly
5. A shape with three sides and three angles is a triangul. — triangle
6. The Earth can be divided into the Northern and Southern or the Western and Eastern Hemisphere. — Hemisphere
7. Before the team plays in the championship, they must first win the simifinal. — semifinal
8. A unihorn is a fictional animal with one long horn in the center of its forehead. — unicorn
9. People who have a hard time seeing both near and far may need biphocals: eyeglasses that have lenses to help see both near and far. — bifocals
10. A unicycle is a vehicle with one wheel; a bicycle is a vehicle with two wheels; a tricicle is a vehicle with three wheels. — tricycle

93

94

Write each of the following spelling words on the lines provided. Circle the prefixes **pre-** and **post-**.

1. (pre)arrange   **prearrange**   4. (post)date   **postdate**
2. (pre)caution   **precaution**   5. (post)pone   **postpone**
3. (pre)heat   **preheat**   6. (post)war   **postwar**

Complete the following letter with words from above.

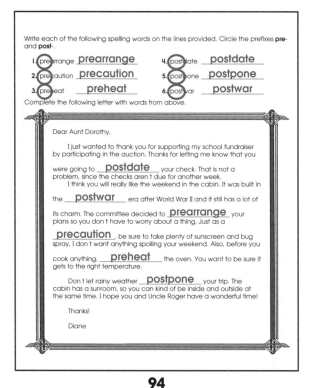

Dear Aunt Dorothy,

I just wanted to thank you for supporting my school fundraiser by participating in the auction. Thanks for letting me know that you were going to __postdate__ your check. That is not a problem, since the checks aren t due for another week.

I think you will really like the weekend in the cabin. It was built in the __postwar__ era after World War II and it still has a lot of its charm. The committee decided to __prearrange__ your plans so you don t have to worry about a thing. Just as a __precaution__, be sure to take plenty of sunscreen and bug spray, I don t want anything spoiling your weekend. Also, before you cook anything, __preheat__ the oven. You want to be sure it gets to the right temperature.

Don t let rainy weather __postpone__ your trip. The cabin has a sunroom, so you can kind of be inside and outside at the same time. I hope you and Uncle Roger have a wonderful time!

Thanks!

Diane

95

Write the meaning of each prefix below.

1. im-   **not**   5. hemi-   **half**
2. uni-   **one**   6. bi-   **two**
3. tri-   **three**   7. semi-   **half**
4. in-   **not**

Write each of the following spelling words. Circle the prefixes.

1. (im)balance   **imbalance**   7. (hemi)sphere   **hemisphere**
2. (im)measurable   **immeasurable**   8. (semi)annual   **semiannual**
3. (im)proper   **improper**   9. (uni)verse   **universe**
4. (in)accurate   **inaccurate**   10. (bi)weekly   **biweekly**
5. (in)decisive   **indecisive**   11. (bi)noculars   **binoculars**
6. (in)direct   **indirect**   12. (tri)angle   **triangle**

Unscramble the spelling words and write them on the lines provided.

1. There is an lanebimac __imbalance__ in strength between the two wrestlers.
2. Our seats were so far away, we had to use olarbcusni __binoculars__ to see the game.
3. The bill for dinner is curanitane __innacurate__ and is being corrected.
4. The student council meets wekeylib __biweekly__ in the meeting room.
5. The ways the volunteers helped at the bake sale were marsibelameu __immeasurable__.
6. The angles of a gnitarle __triangle__ equal 180 degrees.

96

Say each of the following words out loud. Then, write each word on the lines provided.

Spelling Tip	A **suffix** is a group of letters that is added to the end of a base word to change its meaning. The suffix **-ate** means *the state or quality of.* The suffix **-ive** means **inclined to**. The suffix **-ship** means *the state or quality of or the skill or art of.*

Spelling Words

activate	**activate**
constructive	**constructive**
championship	**championship**
communicate	**communicate**
creative	**creative**
friendship	**friendship**
considerate	**considerate**
effective	**effective**
hardship	**hardship**
fortunate	**fortunate**
impressive	**impressive**
leadership	**leadership**
separate	**separate**
inventive	**inventive**
relationship	**relationship**

97

Words in Context

Complete the following biography with spelling words. The first letter of each word has been given for you. Not all of the words are used. You will not repeat any of the words. Use a dictionary if you need help.

Martin Luther King, Jr.

One of America s greatest figures, Martin Luther King, Jr., born in Atlanta, Georgia, in 1929, is best known as one of America s greatest civil rights leaders.

In 1955, Martin Luther King, Jr. led the boycott of segregated bus lines in Montgomery, Alabama. The buses kept people of different races s__eparate__.

An i__mpressive__ victory followed in 1956 when Montgomery, Alabama, desegregated their busses. King s philosophy included nonviolent resistance. Such protests became a c__onstructive__ method in gaining recognition of injustices and served to a__ctivate__ thousands of people to march for justice. His l__eadership__ in civil rights and nonviolent resistance to end racial prejudice earned him the Nobel Peace Prize in 1964.

King s concerns also turned to those who faced one h__ardship__ after another, such as the poor. Martin Luther King was assassinated in 1968.

Those who were f__ortunate__ enough to hear him speak knew he had a c__reative__ and e__ffective__ ability to c__ommunicate__ to the public. King is considered a national hero and peacemaker.

Answer Key

Page 98

Fun with Words
Choose the correct spelling word that describes each illustration.

1. Our team is the victor. We won the __championship__

2. I believe I m connected to you somehow. I think we are brothers. We have a __relationship__.

3. The four of us are pals. Over the years, we have formed a great __friendship__

4. I love to make and create things that did not exist before. I am __inventive__.

5. My teacher is kind and thoughtful. You could say she is the most __considerate__ person I know.

Words Across the Curriculum
Write the social studies words on the lines beside each word.

1. delicate __delicate__   3. positive __positive__

2. negative __negative__   4. protective __protective__

Complete the following paragraph with words from above.

Endangered species are animals and plants whose existance are in danger due to several different factors, such as chemical pollution and the loss of habitats.

However, the news is not completely __negative__. Some organizations are having a __positive__ impact in helping endangered species. Wildlife conservation groups are working to establish __protective__ habitats that stabilize the __delicate__ balance of life.

98

Page 99

Words in Writing
Write a biography about a historic figure. Use at least five words from this lesson.

Answers will vary.

Using the Dictionary
Some words can serve as more than one part of speech, such as nouns, verbs, adjectives, or adverbs. The dictionary will tell you the different parts of speech (usually an abbreviation, such as **n** for *noun*) and provide the definition for each. Look up the following words in a dictionary. Write all of the parts of speech listed for each word.

1. activate	v		11. impressive	adj	
2. constructive	adj		12. leadership	n	
3. championship	n		13. separate	v; adj	
4. communicate	v		14. inventive	adj	
5. creative	adj		15. relationship	n	
6. friendship	n		16. delicate	adj	
7. considerate	adj		17. negative	adj; n	
8. effective	adj		18. positive	adj; n	
9. hardship	n		19. protective	adj	
10. fortunate	adj				

99

Page 100

Say each of the following words out loud. Then, write each word on the lines provided.

Spelling Tip	The suffixes -**able** and -**ible** both mean *inclined to.*

Spelling Words

believable	believable
comfortable	comfortable
comparable	comparable
memorable	memorable
predictable	predictable
reasonable	reasonable
reliable	reliable
valuable	valuable
washable	washable
convertible	convertible
divisible	divisible
invincible	invincible
responsible	responsible
sensible	sensible
visible	visible

100

Page 101

Words in Context
Complete the following paragraph with spelling words. The first letter of each word has been given for you. Not all of the words will be used. You will not use words more than once.

Mayan Pyramids

While they may not be c__omparable__ to the famous Egyptian pyramids,

the pyramids of Mexico are just as m__emorable__. The Maya is an ancient tribe from southern Mexico and Central America. Their civilization formed around 1500 B.C.

The Mayas built seemingly i__nvincible__ pyramids. Some pyramids were built to be climbed, with burial plots on top. Some were built to be sacred, without stairs, never to be climbed. Many of them also served as observatories, as the Maya were interested in the stars and planets.

The city of Palenque was located in a dense rainforest. The pyramids and other buildings there were built against a hill so they could be v__isible__ at great distances through the forest. The city of Tikal is now located in the middle of a wildlife preserve. This area of land is quite v__aluable__ to the many birds and animals that live there, some of which are endangered.

Mayans were a s__ensible__ and organized people. Using mathematics, solar eclipses were p__redictable__. At the city of Uaxact n, the Maya built a r__eliable__ solar observatory that included a pyramid and three temples. Mayan pyramids were impressive and functional. They reveal the intelligent and skilled characteristics of the ancient Mayans.

101

Answer Key

Answer Key

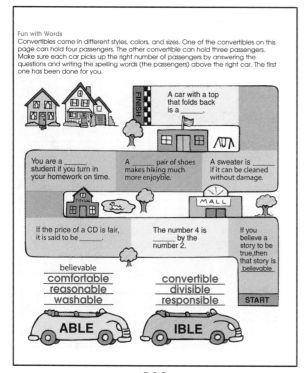

102

Words in Writing
Create a game by writing questions using spelling words. The questions must be answered correctly in order for players to advance. Be creative and have fun!

Answers will vary.

Misspelled Words
The following narrative contains misspelled spelling words. Cross out the misspelled words and write them correctly above the misspelled word.

visible
The sun was ~~visible~~ coming up over the mountain as the hikers started their day.
reliable   sensible   comfortable
The ~~relyable~~ guides had advised them to be ~~sensable~~ and pack ~~comfrtble~~ shoes and
clothing. The day was warm, so they brought plenty of water. The trail was hilly and the
                                                                    invincible
hikers were exhilarated by the vigorous exercise. It made them feel ~~invincble~~.
Throughout the day, they saw unbelievable wildlife. They wrote in their journals about the
foxes, coyotes, deer, and varied birds and squirrels they saw. Seeing animals in their own
                        responsible
habitat made them feel ~~responsable~~ for taking care of the environment. By the end of
                                                                    predictable
the day they were exhausted but inspired. The day had not been ~~predictble~~ at all,
memorable   valuable
with ~~memorble~~ surprises at every turn. The trip was a truly ~~valuable~~ experience.

103

Say each of the following words out loud. Then, write each word on the lines provided.

Spelling Tip	The noun suffixes **-ance** and **-ence** both mean *the state or quality of*. The adjective suffixes **-ant** and **-ent** both mean *inclined to*.

Spelling Words

appearance	appearance
distance	distance
entrance	entrance
performance	performance
confidence	confidence
excellence	excellence
independence	independence
contestant	contestant
hesitant	hesitant
ignorant	ignorant
pleasant	pleasant
consistent	consistent
intelligent	intelligent
persistent	persistent
urgent	urgent

104

Words in Context
Complete the following passage with spelling words.

Jubilee!

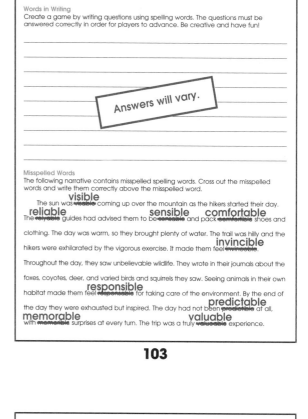

Each **contestant** anxiouisly awaited the start of the quiz show. The three middle school students had been working all year for the opportunity to show off their skills.

This would be their first **appearance** on television. Each contestant knew that he or she was **intelligent**, but there could only be one winner.

Their coaches had been **persistent** about what and how much the contestants studied. Rest was important, too. The coaches reminded them that some contestants are **ignorant** to the fact that starting a competition with a clear, rested mind can be just as vital as knowing the material.
Winning this competition could bring the winner some financial **independence**. A college scholarship would be awarded to the winner. Thinking about that was really getting their stomachs tied in knots.
Finally, the sound of the host introducing the show could be heard back stage. The contestants names were called. They wished each other luck and walked toward the stage, ready to make their big **entrance**.

Word Building
For the following nouns, write the words in their adjective forms. For the adjectives, write their noun forms. Use a dictionary if you need help. The first one has been done for you.

Nouns	Adjectives	Adjectives	Nouns
1. distance	distant	1. hesitant	hesitance
2. confidence	confidant	2. ignorant	ignorance
3. excellence	excellent	3. intelligent	intelligence
4. independence	independent	4. persistent	persistence

105

106

Fun with Words
Answer the questions for each contestant with spelling words.

Contestant #1

Contestant #2

Contestant #3

Question 1: noun: What is the length of a line between two points?

distance

Question 1: adjective: What else could an enjoyable day be called?

pleasant

Question 1: noun: What is something or someone that exhibits greatness?

excellence

Question 2: adjective: What is something that demands a quick action?

urgent

Question 2: noun: What is the act of presenting, especially in front of an audience?

performance

Question 2: adjective: What is something or someone that refuses to give up?

persistent

Words Across the Curriculum
Write the science words on the lines beside each word.

1. accidents **accidents**
2. coincidence **coincidence**
3. occurrences **occurrences**
4. sequence **sequence**

The words above are scrambled in the following paragraph. Rewrite the words correctly.

A coincidence is a qucesene **sequence** of events that occur at the same time and that may or may not be connected. Mark Twain was born on the day that Halley's comet appeared. He died on the day that it reappeared. Harriet Tubman, a leader in the struggle against slavery, died on the same day that Rosa Parks, a leader in the Civil Rights Movement, was born. Are these and other crencescucer **occurrences** cenitacds **accidents** ? Some people believe in random acts of cedoneicici **coincidence** . Others believe that there is a reason for why everything happens. What do you believe?

107

Words in Writing
Write a paragraph about a contest you have been in or a contest you have seen. Use at least five words from this lesson.

Answers will vary.

Using the Dictionary
Look up the following words in a dictionary. Rewrite the words and then write a brief definition of each word.

1. appearance **appearance**
2. contestant **contestant**
3. entrance **entrance**
4. ignorant **ignorant**
5. independence **independence**
6. intelligent **intelligent**
7. occurrence **occurrence**
8. sequence **sequence**

Answers will vary depending on dictionaries used. Accept all reasonable answers.

108

Write each of the following spelling words on the lines provided. Circle the suffixes.

1. communicate **communicate**
2. effective **effective**
3. predictable **predictable**
4. valuable **valuable**
5. performance **performance**
6. contestant **contestant**
7. inventive **inventive**
8. relationship **relationship**
9. responsible **responsible**
10. visible **visible**
11. persistent **persistent**
12. excellence **excellence**

Complete the following sentences with spelling words that have the suffixes -ate, -ive, and -ship. Then, answer the questions.

1. Having a good **relationship** with a pet is an enriching part of life. Describe one that you have.

Answers will vary.

2. What is your favorite way to **communicate** : by telephone, letter, email, or face to face?

Answers will vary.

3. Completing homework before dinner can be an **effective** study habit. Do you have a good study habit?

Answers will vary.

4. Someone is **inventive** when they have a new idea or make something for the first time. Give an example how you have done this.

Answers will vary.

109

Complete the following sentences with spelling words that have the suffixes -able and -ible from page 108. Then, answer the questions.

1. The movie was **predictable** ; the audience knew the ending ten minutes after the movie began. What movie have you seen that had this same quality?

Answers will vary.

2. The lake was **visible** from her kitchen window. What can you see from the windows in your classroom?

Answers will vary.

3. The daughter's bracelet was **valuable** because her father gave it to her. What means a lot to you?

Answers will vary.

4. The children and their parents were **responsible** for their new puppy. How have you shown that you are trustworthy and capable?

Answers will vary.

Complete the following sentences with spelling words that have the suffixes -ance, -ence, -ant, and -ent from page 108. Then, answer the questions.

1. A **contestant** takes part in a game or race. What is your favorite game or race?

Answers will vary.

2. If someone doesn't give up, then he or she is **persistent** . Have you been this way?

Answers will vary.

3. What is your favorite **performance** : acting, singing, playing a musical instrument, or something else?

Answers will vary.

4. The winner of the vocabulary bee showed **excellence** in the subject. What is your favorite subject in school?

Answers will vary.

Answer Key

Say each of the following words out loud. Then, write each word on the lines provided.

Spelling Tip	**Homophones** are words that sound exactly the same but are spelled differently and have different meanings.

Spelling Words

leak	leak
leek	leek
canvas	canvas
canvass	canvass
patience	patience
patients	patients
presence	presence
presents	presents
sail	sail
sale	sale
scene	scene
seen	seen
their	their
there	there
they re	they re

110

Words in Context

Complete the following sentences with the correct homophone form the spelling word list.

1. I bought two muffins and lemonade at the bake ____ **sale** ____.
2. Using a ____ **canvas** ____ bag to grocery shop is good for the environment.
3. The doctor has many ____ **patients** ____ to see.
4. Lynn and Leigh are sisters, and ____ **they re** ____ best friends.
5. I think the faucet has a ____ **leak** ____.
6. The actors rehearsed the same ____ **scene** ____ for hours.
7. Haley and Hannah are playing soccer today. I m going to go watch ____ **their** ____ game.
8. I love to go out on the lake and ____ **sail** ____ in the summertime.
9. In order to be effective, teachers must have a lot of ____ **patience** ____.
10. Have you ____ **seen** ____ the play yet?
11. On Saturday, we plan to ____ **canvass** ____ the neighborhood to raise money for the tornado victims.
12. The oranges were left here and the bananas were left over ____ **there** ____.
13. How many ____ **presents** ____ did you get for your birthday?
14. A ____ **leek** ____, a vegetable in the onion family, would work well in that recipe.
15. Your ____ **presence** ____ is required at the meeting.

111

Fun with Words

Each of the following pictures represents one of the homophones from the spelling word list. Identify each of the pictures by writing the homophone on the line provided.

1. presents   3. patients   5. scene

2. sail   4. leek

Words Across the Curriculum

Write the science homophones on the lines beside each word.

1. tide ____ **tide** ____   3. vane ____ **vane** ____
2. tied ____ **tied** ____   4. vein ____ **vein** ____

Complete each of the following sentences with a homophone from above. Use a dictionary if you need help defining a word.

1. The weather ____ **vane** ____ indicates a windy day ahead.
2. The ____ **tide** ____ will be rolling in soon.
3. Let s make sure the boats are all ____ **tied** ____ to the dock.
4. A ____ **vein** ____ is a vessel that carries our blood.

112

Words in Writing

Write a paragraph about a piece of art you would like to create. Use four spelling words in your paragraph.

Answers will vary.

Misspelled Words

Cross out the misspelled word in each sentence and rewrite the word correctly.

1. The ~~lek~~ in the shower is driving me crazy.   **leak**
2. The sails were made of a strong, heavy ~~canvas~~   **canvas**
3. The long training runs required a lot of ~~patients~~, but success at the track meet made it all worth it.   **patience**
4. I m going to add a ~~leke~~ to my salad.   **leek**
5. The students were told to ~~canvas~~ the area and hang up the bake sale fliers.   **canvass**
6. The ~~pachents~~ in the hospital were grateful for their visitors.   **patients**

113

Page 114

Say each of the following words out loud. Then, write each word on the lines provided.

Spelling Tip	Some pairings of words are related both in spelling and meaning.

Spelling Words

fact	fact
factual	factual
harmony	harmony
harmonious	harmonious
human	human
humane	humane
major	major
majority	majority
muscle	muscle
muscular	muscular
nature	nature
natural	natural
produce	produce
production	production
unite	unite
unity	unity

114

Page 115

Words in Context

Complete the following paragraph with spelling words. Use a dictionary if you need help defining the words.

Living Together

The _____fact_____ is, as the world s population increases, the places that a _____human_____ being chooses to live moves more into the woods and forests. These areas are homes to other creatures. Many different kinds of animals that live in _____nature_____ and call these outlying areas home.

As human beings push farther into the animals habitats, the animals are moving into areas populated by human beings. Is there any chance we can all live in _____harmony_____? It is up to the human beings to find a _____harmonious_____ balance for existence. Destroying the animals is not the answer. Some believe that is not _____humane_____, and for the most part, it doesn t even solve the problem.

Eliminating some species upsets the _____natural_____ environmental balance. Forcing some animals into extinction may eliminate the natural balance. Therefore, some animals may become extinct while others _____produce_____ more.

So, what are the answers to living in _____unity_____? One _____major_____ answer is through education. People are becoming more educated on how to coexist with wild animals. Human beings are learning to respect and admire wild animals. With work, it is possible for human beings and animals to coexist and _____unite_____.

115

Page 116

Fun with Words

Complete the following sentences by using the code and filling in the blanks with spelling words.

1=A	4=D	7=G	10=J	13=M	16=P	19=S	22=V	25=Y
2=B	5=E	8=H	11=K	14=N	17=Q	20=T	23=W	26=Z
3=C	6=F	9=I	12=L	15=O	18=R	21=U	24=X	

1. After the strenuous workout, my right calf was sore.
m u s c l e
13 21 19 3 12 5

2. The students read a report that gave many statistics.
f a c t u a l
6 1 3 20 21 1 12

3. The theater department is putting on a major
p r o d u c t i o n in the spring.
16 18 15 4 21 3 20 9 15 14

4. The m a j o r i t y of the students voted in
13 1 10 15 18 9 20 25
the election of the class president.

5. The horses were strong and m u s c u l a r
13 21 19 3 21 12 1 18

Words Across the Curriculum

Write the language arts words on the lines beside each word.

1. poems _____poems_____   3. poetic _____poetic_____

2. poetry _____poetry_____

Complete the sentences with words from above.

1. The _____poems_____ in this book are some of my favorites.

2. _____Poetry_____ is one of my favorite topics to study in language arts.

3. Although not a poem, your letter sounded very _____poetic_____.

116

Page 117

Words in Writing

Write a poem about an animal of your choosing. Use at least three of the words from this lesson.

Answers will vary.

Using the Dictionary

Use a dictionary to look up the differences between the following pairs of words. Rewrite the word, then write its part of speech (**n** for *noun* and **adj** for *adjective*) and a brief definition.

1. fact   word: _____   part of speech _____

   definition: _____

2. factual   word: _____   part of speech _____

   definition: _____

3. human   word: _____

   definition: _____

Answers may vary depending on dictionaries used. Accept all reasonable answers.

4. humane   word: _____

   definition: _____

5. muscle   word: _____   part of speech _____

   definition: _____

6. muscular   word: _____   part of speech _____

   definition: _____

117

Page 118

Say each of the following words out loud. Then, write each word on the lines provided.

Spelling Tip
Most English words were created and developed from other languages. Many English words have Latin and Greek roots. Knowing what the roots mean can help you know what the English word means.

Spelling Words

autobiography	autobiography
autograph	autograph
automatic	automatic
megaphone	megaphone
microphone	microphone
saxophone	saxophone
symphony	symphony
telephone	telephone
telecast	telecast
telescope	telescope
export	export
import	import
passport	passport
portable	portable
transport	transport

Page 119

Words in Context
Each root has a specific meaning that gives us clues to the meanings of the words themselves.

Greek root: **auto**   meaning: *self or same*
Greek root: **phone**   meaning: *sound*
Greek root: **tele**   meaning: *distant*
Latin root: **port**   meaning: *to carry*

Complete the following sentences with spelling words. Use the meanings of the roots to help you.

1. If one writes the story of one's own life, he or she is writing an **autobiography**.
2. This large cone-shaped tube, called a **megaphone**, sends a person's voice farther when one speaks into it.
3. A **telecast** sends a broadcast through air waves.
4. To carry goods out of one country to another is to **export** the goods.
5. When celebrities sign an **autograph**, they are signing their own name.
6. An electronic device that magnifies sounds is called a **microphone**.
7. Astronomers use a **telescope** to make distant objects seem closer.
8. To bring goods in from another country is to **import** the goods.
9. If something moves or works by itself, then it has an **automatic** operation.
10. A musical instrument that makes sound is a **saxophone**.
11. A **passport** allows travelers to go in and out of other countries.
12. A **symphony** is a long piece of music for a full orchestra.
13. If something is easily carried it is said to be **portable**.
14. Trains, planes, and ships often carry, or **transport**, goods from one place to another.
15. **Telephone** combines two Greek roots, one meaning *distant* and one meaning *sound*.

Page 120

Fun with Words
Write each of the spelling words on the legs of the appropriate web. One word will go on two different webs.

port: export, import, passport, portable, transport, telecast

tele: telephone, telecast, telescope

auto: autobiography, autograph, automatic

phone: megaphone, microphone, saxophone, symphony, telephone

Words Across the Curriculum
Write the history words on the lines beside each word.

1. automobiles **automobiles**   3. telegraph **telegraph**
2. telegram **telegram**

Complete each sentence with a history word.

1. It seems like most of the mail we receive today is electronic mail. But how did people get mail before planes, trains, and **automobiles**?
2. The pony express operated in 1860 and 1861 between Missouri and California. The **telegraph**, which sends messages by a code of electrical signals, came into existence in 1861.
3. The **telegram** is the name of the messages that were sent by a system of electrical signals.

Page 121

Words in Writing
Choose two words from each of the Latin and Greek root groups: **auto, phone, tele,** and **port**. Write a short paragraph about an inventor you admire.

Answers will vary.

Misspelled Words
The following dialogue contains misspelled spelling words. Cross out the incorrect words and write them correctly above the misspelled words.

telephone
The ~~telefone~~ rang and rang. It must have been important. On the last ring, Theo burst through the door.

Oh, no, I missed it, he groaned. He quickly dialed the number to get messages.

symphony
Yes, it's from the ~~symfony~~ yes yes yes, I got in! Theo was shouting throughout the house, even though nobody else was home yet.

What are you in? asked Theo's dad as he walked through the back door.

megaphone
You're shouting so loud it sounds like you're screaming through a ~~megafone~~.

saxophone   **symphony**
I'm the newest ~~saxofone~~ player in the community junior ~~symfony~~, shouted Theo.

Well, congratulations! Theo's dad said as he gave him a big hug.

automatic
You know being accepted isn't ~~automatic~~, I practiced a lot, stated Theo.

autograph
I know! Can I have your ~~autograf~~ now? Theo's dad asked.

Answer Key

Say each of the following words out loud. Then, write each word on the lines provided.

Spelling Words

access	access
excess	excess
choose	choose
chose	chose
finally	finally
finely	finely
later	later
latter	latter
medal	medal
metal	metal
personal	personal
personnel	personnel
recent	recent
resent	resent
sense	sense
since	since

122

Words in Context
Complete the following sentences with spelling words.

1. Dylan has wanted to be a marine biologist __since__ she was a little girl.
2. Do you think this road will give us __access__ to the park?
3. Between pizza and pasta, Mitzi prefers the __latter__.
4. The person in charge of hiring is called the __personnel__ director.
5. Can we __choose__ two or three side dishes to go along with the entr e?
6. The __recent__ storms left the town without electricity for two days.
7. __Finally__, the rain ended, and we could finish the baseball game.
8. If you eat the whole pizza you will definitely be eating to __excess__.
9. The art sculpture was made of __metal__.
10. Does it make __sense__ to start the project now?
11. After we have eaten, let s go to the __later__ showing of the movie.
12. Greg __chose__ to work on his history homework before his math.
13. Louis won the first place __medal__ in the science fair.
14. Leigh __resent__ the fax when it didn t appear to go through the first time.
15. The chef __finely__ chopped the vegetables.

Word Building
The prefix **re-** means *again* or *back*. The suffix **-ly** means *having the attribute of*. Add the prefix to the first word and the suffix to the second word. Then, write the definition for new each word.

1. appear __reappear__ __to appear again__
2. scholar __scholarly__ __having the attribute of a scholar.__

123

Fun with Words
Find and circle each spelling word in the puzzle below. They can be horizontal, vertical, forward, backward, or diagonal. Once you have found them, write them on the lines next to the puzzle.

1. excess
2. personal
3. metal
4. finely
5. finally
6. latter
7. access
8. sense
9. since
10. resent
11. later
12. recent
13. choose
14. personnel
15. chose
16. medal

124

Words in Writing
Write about a time when you exercised too long or stayed up too late. How did you feel afterward? Would you do this same thing again?

Answers will vary.

Using the Dictionary
Use a dictionary to look up the definitions of the following pairs of words. Rewrite each word and then write a brief definition for each.

1. access: __access__
2. excess: __excess__
3. later: __later__
4. latter: __latter__
5. medal: __medal__
6. metal: __metal__
7. recent: __recent__
8. resent: __resent__
9. sense: __sense__
10. since: __since__

Answers may vary depending on dictionaries used. Accept all reasonable answers.

125

Spectrum Spelling
Grade 6

Answer Key

127

The various parts of speech of the entry word will also be given the plurals of nouns, tenses of verbs, and comparatives and superlatives of adjectives.

Sometimes, even a picture will be given to help illustrate an entry word.

A **thesaurus** is also a valuable reference tool, providing synonyms and antonyms for the entry word.

A thesaurus is set up just like a dictionary, with each entry word listed alphabetically and guide words at the top of each page. Each entry word will list its part of speech and then synonyms for that word. Some thesauruses will even have sample sentences using the entry word. There will also be a list of antonyms for the entry word.

A thesaurus is particularly useful when writing. Using synonyms and antonyms will make writing more lively with more variety.

Place these words in alphabetical order. Then, look them up in the dictionary. Write each word, their pronunciations, parts of speech, and definitions on the lines provided. If a word has more than one part of speech, write the part of speech and definition for the first listed.

animal	audience	teamwork	harmony	telescope
historical	compassion	postscript	cartoon	medal

1. word **animal**   pronunciation **an ə mel**
   part of speech **n**   definition **living beings that move, have sense organs**

2. word **audience**   pronunciation **dē ens**
   part of speech **n**   definition **a group of people gathered to hear a performance**

3. word **cartoon**   pronunciation **k r t n**
   part of speech **n**   definition **a drawing in a newspaper or magazine that is often humorous**

128

4. word **compassion**   pronunciation **kem pash en**
   part of speech **n**   definition **a feeling of wanting to help others or having sympathy**

5. word **harmony**   pronunciation **h r mə nē**
   part of speech **n**   definition **peace and friendship and agreement of ideas and feelings**

6. word **historical**   pronunciation **his t r i kel**
   part of speech **adj**   definition **what existed in history**

7. word **medal**   pronunciation **med əl**
   part of speech **n**   definition **a metal object with words or a design that is given as an honor**

8. word **postscript**   pronunciation **post skript**
   part of speech **n**   definition **a note added below a signature or at the end of a book**

9. word **teamwork**   pronunciation **tēm wurk**
   part of speech **n**   definition **the effort of people working as a group**

10. word **telescope**   pronunciation **tel ə skōp**
    part of speech **n**   definition **an instrument that makes distant objects seem closer**

129

Look up the following words in a thesaurus. Write one synonym and one antonym (if one is given) for each word. Then, write a sentence using the synonym in one sentence and the antonym in another.

1. athletic   synonym _____   antonym _____
   synonym sentence _____
   antonym sentence _____

2. friendship   synonym _____   antonym _____
   synonym sentence _____
   antonym sentence _____

3. informal   synonym _____   antonym _____
   synonym sentence _____
   antonym sentence _____

4. memorable   synonym _____
   synonym sentence _____
   antonym sentence _____

Answers will vary.

5. scenic   synonym _____   antonym _____
   synonym sentence _____
   antonym sentence _____

6. visible   synonym _____   antonym _____
   synonym sentence _____
   antonym sentence _____

130

Write each of the following spelling words on the lines provided.

1. leak **leak**   6. factual **factual**
2. leek **leek**   7. nature **nature**
3. presence **presence**   8. natural **natural**
4. presents **presents**   9. unite **unite**
5. fact **fact**   10. unity **unity**

Choose five spelling words from above and write them in alphabetical order. Then, use a dictionary to write their pronunciations, parts of speech, and definitions.

1. word _____   pronunciation _____
   part of speech _____   definition _____

2. word _____   pronunciation _____
   part of speech _____   definition _____

3. word _____   pronunciation _____
   part of speech _____

Answers will vary.

4. word _____   pronunciation _____
   part of speech _____   definition _____

5. word _____   pronunciation _____
   part of speech _____   definition _____

Answer Key

Write each of the following spelling words on the lines provided.

1. autograph **autograph**
2. automatic **automatic**
3. portable **portable**
4. transport **transport**
5. finely **finely**

6. later **later**
7. latter **latter**
8. medal **medal**
9. personal **personal**
10. recent **recent**

Choose seven spelling words from above and write them in alphabetical order. Then, look them up in a thesaurus and write one synonym and one antonym for each.

1. word _____   synonym _____
   antonym _____

2. word _____   synonym _____
   antonym _____

3. word _____   synonym _____
   antonym _____

4. word _____
   antonym _____

Answers will vary.

5. word _____   synonym _____
   antonym _____

6. word _____   synonym _____
   antonym _____

7. word _____   synonym _____
   antonym _____

131

Notes

Notes

Notes

Notes

Notes